The

Cat
ENCYCLOPEDIA

ANIWA
PUBLISHING

ROYAL CANIN

Contributors

SCIENTIFIC ADVISORS

PROFESSOR BERNARD-MARIE PARAGON,
National Veterinary School of Alfort,
President, French Society of Feline Science

JEAN-PIERRE VAISSAIRE,
Doctor of Veterinary Medicine

And in alphabetical order:

Bacqué	Hélène	UMES – National Veterinary School of Alfort
Beugnet	Frédéric	Lecturer – National Veterinary School of Alfort
Biourge	Vincent	D.V.M. – Royal Canin Research Center
Blanchard	Géraldine	D.V.M. – National Veterinary School of Alfort
Bossé	Philippe	Professor – National Veterinary School of Alfort
Bullard-Cordeau	Brigitte	Editor-in-chief – Animal Junior
Casteran	Martine	Editor-in-chief – Atout Chat
Chatelain	Éliane	Professor – National Veterinary School of Lyon
Chaurand	Jean-Paul	D.V.M. – National Veterinary School of Alfort
Crépin	Fabrice	D.V.M. – Royal Canin
Déboise	Mikael	Researcher – Royal Canin Research Center
Fortamps	Béatrice	Editorial Coordinator – Diffomédia
Fradin-Ferme	Michèle	D.V.M. – Clinical Practitioner
Gagnon	Anne-Claire	D.V.M. – Vice President, French Society of Feline Science
Ganivet	Alain	D.V.M. – Clinical Practitioner
Garcia	Catherine	Training Director, Feline Science – Royal Canin
Gogny	Marc	Professor – National Veterinary School of Nantes
Grandjean	Dominique	Lecturer – National Veterinary School of Alfort
Guillot	Jacques	Lecturer – National Veterinary School of Alfort
Hugues	François	D.V.M. – Journalist, Europe 1
Kretz	Catherine	D.V.M. – Secretary, French Society of Feline Science
Lagarde	Henri	Chief Executive Officer – Royal Canin
Levesque	Anne	Research Center – Royal Canin
Moraillon	Anne	D.V.M. – National Veterinary School of Alfort
Morris	James G.	Professor – University of California, Davis
Pibot	Pascale	D.V.M. – Royal Canin Research Center
Pierson	Philippe	D.V.M. – Royal Canin
Samaille	Jean-Pierre	D.V.M. – Journalist, L'Action Vétérinaire
Soriano	Bruno	Journalist – Chat magazine
Vaissaire	Josée	D.V.M. – Member, Veterinary Academy of France

Publishing Managment
BERNARDO GALLITELLI,
Chief Executive Officer
Aniwa S.A.

GUY ROLLAND
Aniwa Publishing

"The smallest feline is a masterpiece."

LEONARDO DA VINCI

An Invitation to the World of the Cat

The cat, master of the house, so close yet so distant, so familiar yet so mysterious, has always fascinated humans with its looks and behavior.

Long-time inhabitants of the desert and savanna, cats still carry their biological needs and character within, as part of their physiology. Their character, like that of their distant ancestors, is a subtle combination of nonchalance and adventurousness.

From the deserts of yore to the countryside and cities of today, the feline world has changed rapidly:

- in thirty years, the number of feline breeds resulting from planned hybridization conducted by humans has virtually tripled, from some twenty in 1960 to over fifty at the end of the century.
- spectacular scientific knowledge has been acquired recently.

A specialist in premium feline nutrition, Royal Canin has long followed the tracks of this ancient solitary hunter. Major scientific advances of the past few years have brought us beyond the two traditional roles of nutrition (to build and maintain the organism, and to provide energy) and added a third: prevention. The notion of feline nutrition for health has been born.

Because humans domesticated cats, our primary task is to respect cats as animals, to feed them, and to ensure their health and well-being in accordance with their true specific needs, rather than based on our own human projections.
This is the approach of Royal Canin, a manufacturer specializing in premium feline nutrition which has always followed this ethic of true respect for the animal.

We hope this encyclopedia will help you discover a fascinating world rich with a long history and enhanced by the most recent scientific findings.

Thank you to all who contributed to creating this work: researchers at veterinary schools in France and abroad, as well as at the Royal Canin Research Center, under the direction of Professor Paragon and Dr. Vaissaire.

I invite you to explore these pages brimming with images and information and let yourself be swept away by the magical world of the cat, an intermingling of science and fantasy the cat offers us without restraint.

Henri LAGARDE,
Chief Executive Officer
Groupe Royal Canin

Foreword

Cats are not small dogs! Shameless hunters, cats have retained their original characteristics as strict carnivores from their hunting days. This explains why many of us are drawn to this exceptional companion and requires a careful respect for the cat's specific features, which each owner must know. This book is intended to reveal the big and small secrets that make up the cat.

The cohabitation of humans and cats, though it long remained distant, reaches back into the mists of time. The hunting skill of these small felines made them the natural protectors of granaries and kitchens. For this they were truly venerated in ancient Egypt. However, the cat's independence - sometimes bordering on disrespect - and the pagan practices with which cats were associated in the Middle Ages tarnished their image for a long time. Not until the literary salons of the 19th century and the world of artists did the cat come back into fashion. But this comeback was often at the price of the castration of males, a practice considered a means of re-entering the intelligentsia and acquiring a sort of perfection.

In our urban world, domestic cats carry a bit of the magic of the big cats, in their supple back, noble gait, and luminous gaze. We enjoy this and would hate to lose this pleasure. In France, one of every four households has at least one cat. Over eight million little felines will move in with us in the 21st century and, although most of this population might be considered "mixed breed cats," the fascination continues.

Yet another book on cats . . . but a book in which we aimed to combine knowledge, culture, and beauty; a book for an animal food manufacturer with contributions by scientists, writers, breeders, and enlightened cat fanciers. Because scientists are qualified to satisfy the natural curiosity of cat owners, we chose the best scientists for this project so that the basic knowledge gathered up to now could be made accessible to all in simple, precise terms. Because cats have been omnipresent in the world of humans throughout history, we sought proof of this presence in all forms of art and media. Because cats and beauty are closely intertwined, we aimed to gather the most beautiful illustrations in this book.

Sincere thanks to all who contributed to the technical, scientific, and aesthetic success of this work, particularly to my colleagues from the French Society of Feline Science. Our best reward will be the pleasure you find in exploring these pages and extracting the information that will help you better understand—and better love—your feline companion.

Professor B.-M. PARAGON,
President, French Society of Feline Science

Preface

Over eight million cats currently live in France. In the past decade, we made significant strides in our knowledge of this companion. For this reason, the project of making all the basic facts about this species accessible to the public, in an educational manner, is especially welcome.

By studying the origins and evolution of domestic cats, we can situate them within the Felids, of which the original type was the wild cat (Felis silvestris) that inhabited the large, Old World forests. Our Felis catus, represented by the many breeds described in the Cat Encyclopedia, is thought to have originated in Egypt from a wild felid living in Libya or eastern Africa.

Egyptian civilization gave the cat a privileged place among the gods. Bastet, the cat goddess of music, dance, and motherhood, appeared in the twenty-second dynasty, during the golden age of Pharaonic civilization.

Today, there are still many cat worshippers. Cat fanciers gather together in associations to work for the greater glory of the cat, although not always in perfect harmony. The merit of the Cat Encyclopedia is that it sums up the growing diversity of breeds and the ever-changing world of cat fancy.

Brought to France in the Middle Ages, the cat has remained highly present in art and the media. The appearance of cats in both pictorial works of the classical period and in works of animal artists of the 19th and 20th centuries shows that artists used these subjects to convey their anguish, joy, and fantasies.

The chapters covering the various aspects of daily life with a cat are of great practical value to the reader. Feline physiology and pathology are now much better understood, thanks to original work demonstrating that, contrary to an opinion long considered dogma, cats cannot be put in the same category as dogs. Cats have different nutritional needs, very different behavior, and, quite often, specific illnesses.

The Cat Encyclopedia, under the talented direction of Professor Bernard-Marie Paragon, brings together contributors who are the authority in their respective fields. They made often complex notions accessible to the general public. There is no doubt that cat lovers—I hesitate to write "owners," so true is it that, while you can own a dog, you instead live in your cat's home, with the cat always retaining a certain degree of independence—will find in this work the information they seek on their favorite animal.

Professor Robert MORAILLON,
Director, National Veterinary School of Alfort

Summary

True
respect
of the
Cat

As forgivable as it may be, treating the cat as if it were a little human being is a biological mistake that may prove to be dangerous for the animal.

Respecting the cat for what it gives us and represents to us should not consist of developing an anthropomorphic approach aiming to make the cat, as we often hear, "a child, if only it could speak". Biology is such that it preferred the earthly diversity of living creatures, making each one of them the complement of the others so as to tend towards a delicate balance that Man may not alter in any way.

This anthropomorphic reflex, as forgivable as it may be, given the sometimes powerful emotions that we all feel towards our cats, must therefore be shunned as being disrespectful of their biological and physiological functioning and, consequently, may prove to be dangerous to them.

The best examples of this reality may be found in the daily diet

• Man can change his diet at each mealtime without problems ... but, if his digestive system were designed like that of the cat, such continuous dietary variation would give him constant problems with diarrhoea.

• Man needs cooked food, salt, sugar, appetizing smells and presentation of the food on his plate in order to enjoy his meal, but, if his senses were those of the cat, he would need only the merest hint of the latter to appreciate it completely ...

• For thousands of years, man has been able to take his time to eat his meals, without the risk of becoming the prey of a wild predator but, if he were a cat, evolution would have left him with more of

that reflex of rapid consumption imprinted in the genes of all animals likely to have their food stolen by a member of its own species or be attacked by a predator ...

• Man takes his meals at regular intervals (morning, midday, evening), but the cat is originally a lone hunter of desert lands who provides for his dietary needs by a succession of small meals, morning, noon and night (up to 16 a day).

So, with all due deference; cats are cats. They must be appreciated, treated and respected as such. And, if we consider the examples already mentioned, science and observation will only support these facts.

The digestion is a typical example of the reactions and mechanisms proper to each species, any assimilation may prove to be dangerous for the cat (or for humans), the differences being so obvious and the behaviour patterns so dissimilar.

The passage of food in the organism allows a better understanding of these key notions.

Generally speaking, the human digestive system represents 11% of the body weight, compared with only 2.8% to 3.5% for the cat. Hardly surprising to hear that Man is better able to digest the most varied elements.

Food appreciation: smell and taste differently involved

The cat, unlike human beings, appreciates its food first and foremost by smell. The surface of its nasal mucus is 10 times greater than that of humans. A cat's nose contains up to 67 million olfactory receptors, while the most sensitive human nose has no more than 20 million. Taste, however, despite the received wisdom, is only very marginally involved in the cat's food preferences. While humans have some 9 000 "taste buds" (the cells that receive and analyse the taste of food), the cat has 19 times fewer and, once in its mouth, the food does not linger on the tongue but is sent very quickly towards the stomach. The cat, which does not respond particularly to sweet tastes, is a strict carnivore that does not "synthetise" taurine, but finds it exclusively in the flesh of the animals it hunts or in prepared croquettes.

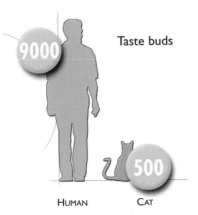

Taste buds

9000

500

HUMAN   CAT

Predigestion: *from the oral cavity to the stomach*

The cat spends very little of its time chewing its food. It eats hastily, whereas humans ready their food for digestion by prolonged chewing, finding pleasure by releasing flavours and, by grinding the food down and mixing it with saliva, and begins the first stage of digestion via the enzymes contained in the latter. For the cat, however, the stomach is the chief location where the processes of digestion are started.

Scientific reality shows us once again: the stomach represents more than 60% of the total weight of the digestive system of the feline species compared with only 11% for humans.

The very acid stomach pH, plus the large amounts of hydrochloric acid (6 times greater than in humans), equips the cat's stomach admirably for its function as a purifier, providing it with an extraordinarily efficient natural barrier against digestive infections.

Weight of digestive tract as percentage of body weight	**11%**	**2,8% to 3,5%**
Surface of nasal mucus	2 à 3 cm²	20 cm²
Olfactory cells	5 to 20 million	60 to 65 million
Taste buds	9 000 buds	500 buds
Dentition	32 teeth	30 teeth
Mastication	prolonged	no chewing
Salivary digestive enzymes	YES	NO
Duration of food intake	1 hour	multiple meals
Stomach capacity	1,3 l	0,3 l
Stomach pH	2 to 4	1 to 2
Length of small intestine	6 to 6,5 m	1 to 1,7 m
Length of large intestine	1,5 m	0,3 to 0,4 m
Density of intestinal flora	10 000 000 bacteria/g	10 000 bacteria/g
Duration of intestinal transit	30 hours to 5 days	12 to 24 hours
Adult glucid requirement	60 to 65% of the dry matter	low
Adult protein requirement	8 to 12% of the dry matter	25 to 40% of the dry matter
Adult lipid requirement	25 to 30% of the dry matter	15 to 45% of the dry matter
Dietary habit	**omnivore**	**carnivore**

Digestive performance: *inherited in the genes*

Originally, the cat is a "nibbler". In fact, if food is left out for it, the cat will make between 10 and 16 snacks a day. The cat also drinks about 10 times a day. Meals last only 2 to 3 minutes. These small quantities spread throughout the day explain why the digestive transit is very rapid in the cat compared with that of humans (12 to 24 hours compared with 30 to 48 hours).

To understand these elements, which may also be considered in other biological functional aspects, is to understand the cat, and above all to accept that the cat is very different to the human, not only in its appearance or in the fact that it cannot "speak". The sometimes-extreme anthropomorphism touted in certain films, for instance, is not only scientifically regrettable, but is actually very harmful and may even reduce the life expectancy of the animal.

The differences between man and cat

*Physiological differences
and differences in basic dietary habit mean
that each has specific nutritional needs.*

Failure to recognize the real needs of the animal, combined with every owner's natural desire to "do the best", may represent a danger to our animals by projecting on to them our wishes, our lifestyles, without taking account of the essential: their animal nature.

Responsible for the domestication of the cat, man has the duty of feeding it according to its true specific needs, and not according to any human projections. The animal is an animal, and in no way a human being as regards its biology. This is the first rule of true respect of the animal. The choice of food best adapted to one's animal must therefore be guided by a dietary approach that is not influenced by one's own eating habits.

Since the dawn of time Man has been an omnivore, blessed with a sense of taste and enjoying variety to dispel boredom, whereas the organism of the cat, a strict carnivore, is adapted to one particular type of food. Although it is sometimes tempting to

apply the rule of diversity to your cat and serve it food more closely resembling a human meal, this would be ill-adapted to its condition or its morphology. Nearly 5 000 years of domestication of the feline race have not succeeded in transforming these strict carnivores into omnivores.

The same applies to all those little pleasures we offer them in the image of those we treat ourselves to. Butter, a spoonful of yoghurt, fish, cheese, ... all these little "extras" disturb the perfectly balanced ration calculated by a nutritionist. Such imbalances may result in intestinal problems and slowly but surely debilitate the animal. We must remain on our guard and curb our anthropomorphic instincts that may harm the good health of our animals.

From "feeding" to "Health Nutrition"

*To enjoy life
as long as possible*

Although death is, and will remain, an inescapable biological process, it is also true that immense progress has been made in medical science, especially on the preventive side of the equation, now ensuring our feline friends a steadily increasing life expectancy.

An extraordinary improvement in nutrition:

In the past 30 years, the foods prepared by animal feed manufacturers for domestic pets have brought about a revolutionary change in the conditions of life of our cats, formerly fed on scraps and leftovers. It has been estimated that cats have acquired nearly 5 years of additional life expectancy in the past 15 years alone.

It is quite probable that the years to come will bring even higher figures, since three major advances have been made in the past 30 years:

• until 1980, a cat was simply "fed" to stop it feeling hungry,

• after 1980, Health Nutrition took its first steps by allowing for 2 parameters: the Age of the animal and its Level of Activity,

• 1997 to 2000 marks the arrival of Health Nutrition with two new dimensions: Prevention and type of Breed. Four parameters were now taken into account: not only Age and Activity, but also Breed and Physiological Condition of the animal.

The four objectives of health nutrition

1 - To build up/sustain the organism
2 - To provide energy
3 - To nourish and to prevent
4 - To nourish and to treat

It is now possible to formulate feeds in the light of clearly identified requirements, according to known and indexed deficiencies that have to be combated, and to specificities discovered along the way as research moves onwards. Scientists now realise that cats do not have to be fed the same way regardless of whether they are kittens, adults, elderly, pregnant or neutered … all of which are elements to take into account in their daily diet.
This realisation is growing daily and allows the development of the simple Feed (feeding to sustain the animal), and the Basic

Nutrition (meeting the nutritional needs of the organism), then going on to Health Nutrition, where a distinction is made between two complementary approaches: "Nourish and Prevent" and "Nourish and Treat".
So, driven by scientific research in veterinary medicine, the traditional concept of nutrition, namely building up/sustaining the organism and providing energy, has transformed in a matter of years to include the dimensions of prevention and, under certain conditions, treatment.

Basic Nutrition (Nutritional Needs of the Organism)

1 - Building up/sustaining the organism:
Amino acids, minerals, trace elements, vitamins, proteins and certain lipids meet the minimum nutritional need to build up and sustain the organism.

Growth, reproduction, muscles, coat...: proteins
Nervous system, skeleton, teeth, blood...: minerals and trace elements
▶ **Sight, reproduction, skeleton, cells ...:** vitamins
Cell membranes: lipids

2 - Providing energy:
Lipids, carbohydrates and, to a lesser extent, proteins give the animal the necessary energy.

▶ **Energy, appetite:** lipids
Energy, digestion: carbohydrates
Non-essential amino acids

Health Nutrition

Nutrition is now - and this is at least one point of convergence between man and catkind - a key aspect of prevention, probably even the most important; this accounts for its being considered as the

first among medicines (as did Hippocrates in antiquity) … and no doubt the gentlest of them all.

3 - Nourish and prevent:
Certain nutrients are integrated in the prevention of risks such as kidney diseases, digestive problems or the effects of old age …

Bone condition: calcium, excess fatty deposits
Kidney problems: reduced phosphorus levels
Digestive problems: addition of "prebiotics", fermentable
▶ fibres encouraging good balance of the intestinal flora, proteins
Premature ageing: vitamins E-C, essential fatty acids, grape and green-tea polyphenols

4 - Nourish and treat:
To aid recovery from certain illnesses, highly specific nutrients will be included in or left out of the food as part of the therapeutic and convalescent processes.

▶ **Kidneys, allergies, heart, obesity, intestines**

"Nutrients" approach and "Ingredients" approach

The "Nutrients" approach: a "nutritional jigsaw puzzle" with fifty pieces.

This presentation of the concept of nutrition in general and health nutrition in particular thus reinforces the distinction between two approaches with regard to the formulation of products for use in animal feeding: the "Nutrients" approach and the "Ingredients" approach.

The **"Nutrients" approach** allows the formulation of a balanced feed by the putting together of a veritable "jigsaw puzzle" of some fifty "nutrients". Each one of them is indispensable for the health of the animal. In the right proportions, the nutrients represent a more of less large part of each piece of the puzzle. This composition makes possible the accomplishment of the four main objectives of Health Nutrition (building up and sustaining the organism,

providing energy, nourishing and preventing, nourishing and treating), taking account of the parameters of Age, Level of Activity, Breed and Physiological Condition. It also meets the real precise and specific needs of each animal.

The **"Ingredients" approach**, on the other hand, is no more than a simple list of standardised elements (or primary alimentary materials if you will) used in the composition of a food preparation, sometimes even with a simple anthropomorphic vision, as if the animal had the palate and the digestive system of a human. It therefore proves to be less precise, and above all disregards the real needs of the animal.

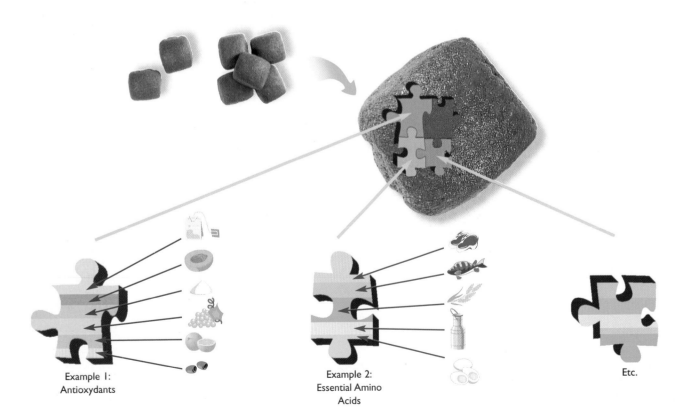

Example 1:
Antioxydants

Example 2:
Essential Amino
Acids

Etc.

Nutrients
or ingredients?
The "Ingredients"
trap

25%
fresh meat

=

4 à 5%
de proteins

How does a feed containing 25% of fresh meat in fact contribute only 4% to 5% of the proteins originating in the fresh meat?

Nourishing a cat properly is therefore a 2-stage operation:

1st stage: a genuine understanding of the animal, its physiology, its biology, its behaviour and, therefore, the real needs of its organism.

2nd stage: an equally scientific approach not only to the nutrients intended to cover these needs, but also to those intended to generate the preventive side - or, as the case may be, the curative side - of the prepared animal feed.

A genuinely nutritional feed is therefore most often a veritable jigsaw puzzle of 50 or 60 essential nutrients (proteins, minerals, vitamins, trace elements, lipids, carbohydrates, …), whereas the seduction of an eye-catching list of "Ingredients" is only very anthropomorphic and serves no real purpose beyond that of flattering the master ("chicken flavour", "lamb", "salmon").

As surprising as it may seem, the protein content of a feed claiming "25% fresh meat" is only between 4% and 5% of the total weight on the dry mat-

ter. In fact, the regulations require the pet food manufacturers to list the ingredients by descending order of weight, before cooking. Fresh meat or certain ingredients containing large amounts of water may therefore be placed at the top of the list, creating the illusion of their being the main source of nutrition.

In the case of a feed claiming to contain 25% lamb, the dry croquette will therefore contain only 4% to 5% of lamb proteins after cooking. Suppose this feed also contains 20% maize, 20% rice, 15% dried fish, 10% poultry fat and 10% vegetable oil. The manufacturer can write "Lamb" in large characters as the main ingredient but, in reality, there is only 4% to 5% lamb proteins, while the cereals are the main ingredients in the finished feed in terms of quantity.

"with beef"	minimum 4% of beef
"with lamb"	minimum 4% of lamb
"with chicken"	minimum 4% of chicken
"rich in beef"	minimum 14% of beef
"rich in lamb"	minimum 14% of lamb

*One feed,
three different
descriptions!*

Dry cat food "with beef" 4% beef

Dry cat food "with lamb" 4% lamb

Dry cat food "with chicken" 4% chicken

*The same ingredients...
the same foodstuffs...
but 3 different names
and 3 different packs*

Another example: the same feed containing, among other ingredients, 4% chicken, 4% lamb and 4% beef may be labelled under three different descriptions: "chicken", "lamb" or "beef". And there will always be someone there to tell you that his animal prefers the lamb version, despite the fact that the actual lamb content is exactly the same as that of the chicken version.

However, this "Ingredients" approach, which has deceived more than one owner, fails to take account of the dosage, quantity, or quality, and of the variety of origins of nutrients - essential to life and adapted to the specific needs of cats - that ensure the quality of a balanced feed. A "standard" feed may, for instance, contain some fifteen nutrients, whereas a "pedigree" or "nutritional" feed will usually contain up to fifty.

Royal Canin, undisputed precursor of feline health nutrition

*Royal Canin: a nutrition concept
that wins the day by uncompromising
fidelity to its roots: "Knowledge and Respect".*

Since its creation, the veterinarians and nutritional experts at Royal Canin have directed their constant efforts towards achieving major advances in terms of canine and feline nutrition. Each year brings its crop of new nutritional programmes and new nutritional formulas that, besides the nutrients essential for maintaining healthy life, also incorporate natural elements to prevent certain diseases and to protect the animal.

1997

First world launch: a new generation of nutritional cat food products (RCFI range), targeted according to the age and physiological condition of the cat (Kitten, Fit , Sensible, Slim, Senior). This new generation resolutely abandoned the traditional anthropomorphic approach based on ingredients ("salmon", "chicken", ...). The RCFI range was an immediate spectacular world-wide success.

1998

First feed developed specifically for castrated males and spayed females at veterinary clinics: Vet Cat, to Nourish and Prevent.

1999

Persian 30: result of the co-operation between R&D and the breeders, the first feed adapted to the physiognomy and the specific nutritional needs of Persian cats:
- development of the Almond 11 croquette,
- Derm system (for a healthy coat and skin care),
- Hairball Transit System (to help eliminate hairballs in the stomach).

2001

World launch of Indoor 27 ®, 1ˢᵗ feed formulated for indoor cats (hairballs, obesity, smell).

2001

V-Diet, to Nourish and Treat, the development of 6 dietary products for cats in particular:
- the hydrolysate for the Hypoallergenic Program,
- the hyperprotein diet for the Obesity Program.

2002

Launch of 4 big world firsts with the new Feline Nutrition range with cats in mind:
- Reinforcement of natural defences (Immunity Program),
- Campaign against cellular ageing (Anti-ageing Complex),
- Regeneration of coat and skin,
- Specially textured croquettes.

2002

Vet Cat Neutered: the first-ever nutritional super-prevention range to cater for the physiological specificities of cats, spayed females and castrated males.

Familiarity breeds respect

To define its products, Royal Canin does not conduct market research or consumer polls, but places the cat, its "one true client", at the centre of operations.
Knowledge of the real nutritional needs of the cat is derived from the daily experience of the partner breeders and the veterinary nutritionists and from the first-hand scientific observations of the Royal Canin Research and Development experts.

An original method allows Royal Canin, more than any other Brand, to be genuinely in the vanguard of innovation and nutritional precision.
A philosophy also based on the sharing of knowledge of the cat through reference works, such as guides to breeding and training and, of course, this Encyclopaedia of the Cat.

ROYAL CANIN

KNOWLEDGE AND RESPECT

THE BREEDS

VOLUME 1

Abyssinian	Maine Coon
American Bobtail	Persian
American Curl	Siamese

VOLUME 2

American Shorthair	Burmese
American Wirehair	Burmilla
Turkish Angora	California Spangled
Balinese	Ceylon
Bengal	Chartreux
Russian Blue	Norwegian Forest Cat
Bombay	Cornish Rex
British Shorthair	

VOLUME 3

Cymric	Javanese
Devon Rex	Korat
European Shorthair	La Perm
Exotic Shorthair	Domestic Lynx
German Rex	Oriental Longhair
Havana	Manx
Japanese Bobtail	

VOLUME 4

Egyptian Mau	Singapura
Munchk	Snowshoe
Ocicat	African Shorthair
Ojos Azules	Somali
Oriental Shorthair	Sphynx
Ragdoll	Tonkinese
Birman	Turkish Van
Scottisch Fold	York Chocolate
Selkirk Rex	Pixie Bob
Siberian Cat	

Egyptian Mau

Country of Origin: Egypt

This spotted cat with lovely mascara markings was deified in ancient times

Mau is the Egyptian word for cat. In fact, the ancestors of this breed were protected, worshipped, and represented on the monuments of ancient Egypt. Nathalie Troubetskoy, a Russian princess exiled in Italy, obtained Egyptian Maus from Cairo in 1953, including a female named Baba and a kitten named Lisa who were shown in Rome in 1955.

In 1956, when the princess emigrated to the United States, she brought her cats and founded the Fatima Cattery. Baba was awarded in 1957. This rapid success encouraged others to breed Egyptian Maus, and the breed was recognized by the C.F.A. and by T.I.C.A., which published a standard in 1988. That same year, the Egyptian Mau was also bred in Europe, where it is still quite uncommon. The F.I.Fe. approved the breed in 1992. The spotted tabby Oriental Shorthair, developed in Britain, is often mistaken for the Egyptian Mau.

BLACK SILVER TABBY

BELOW AND FACING PAGE: BLACK SILVER SPOTTED TABBY

Egyptian Mau

GENERAL
Medium-sized, medium-limbed type, similar to the Abyssinian. Graceful body with well-developed muscles.
Weight: 2.5 to 5 kg. Spotted coat.

Short hair on the inside lying flat. Lynx tips appreciated.

EYES
Large, almond-shaped, neither round nor Oriental type, set at a slight slant. Light green, gooseberry green (▼). Amber is allowed in young adults up to 18 months.

HEAD
Wedge-shaped with slightly rounded contours and no flat surfaces. Slightly rounded forehead. Slight stop or slope between the nose and forehead. The cheeks are not full, except in adult males. Muzzle neither short nor pointed. Nose as long as it is wide.

EARS
Medium to large in size, well-spaced, broad at the base, on alert, and moderately pointed.

COAT
Short, fine, silky, resilient, lying very flat against the body. At least two bands of ticking on the ground color. Coat naturally spotted tabby. Dark, round, evenly spaced spots on the trunk and belly. Stripes on the extremities. "M" or scarab marking on the

SPOTTED TABBY

NECK
Very muscular and arched.

BODY
Moderately long, between foreign and cobby types. High, angular shoulders. Heavy-boned. Very muscular.

LEGS AND PAWS
Hind legs longer than forelegs. Muscular. Small, slightly oval paws.

TAIL
Moderately long, thick at the base, tapering slightly to the tip.

forehead, mascara lines on the cheeks, rings on the tail, broken necklace on the chest, and broken rings on the paws.

VARIETIES
- **silver:** black spots; pale silver ground color; brick red nose; black paw pads
- **bronze:** very dark browns spots; light brown ground color; brick red nose
- **smoke or black smoke:** jet black spots; smoke gray ground color; black nose and paw pads

NOTES
Allowable outcross breeds: none.

FAULTS
Round or short head. Small ears. Full cheeks, except in adult males. Muzzle too pointed or too short. Small, round, or Oriental type eyes. Amber eyes in cats over 18 months old. Massive or Oriental type body. Spots that are touching. Continuous necklaces.

BLACK SILVER SPOTTED TABBY

CHARACTERISTICS
Lively, playful, active, and well-balanced, Egyptian Maus are neither aggressive nor nervous. They do not like agitation. Reserved toward strangers and sociable around other cats, they are gentle and very affectionate toward their owner. They have a soft, pleasant voice.
They can adapt to apartment life but do not tolerate solitude well. A garden lets these athletic hunters blow off steam. They require only weekly brushing.

(▼) F.I.Fe   (■) L.O.O.F.   (★) C.F.A.   (◆) T.I.C.A.

16

Munchk

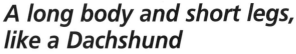

A long body and short legs, like a Dachshund

In 1991 in New York's Madison Square Garden, a strange cat with short legs was shown. It was nicknamed the "Dachshund cat" or "Basset cat." Already by the 1930s, cats of the same type were reported in England but forgotten during World War II. A specimen was described in Stalingrad in 1953.

These cats are named after the inhabitants of Munchkin Land in Fleming's famous movie The Wizard of Oz (1939).

The ancestors of today's Munchkins are descended from Blackberry, a black cat found in Louisiana around 1982.

The gene responsible for short legs, the basis for this spontaneous mutation, is dominant.

T.I.C.A. recognized the breed in 1995 and published a standard the same year. The first Munchkins arrived in France in 1993.

TORTOISESHELL AND WHITE SHORTHAIR

ABOVE:
TORTOISESHELL AND WHITE KITTEN
FACING PAGE:
LONGHAIRED TORTOISESHELL TABBY
AND WHITE

Munchkin

RED AND WHITE

GENERAL
Very short-limbed cat.
Weight: 2.2 to 4 kg.

EYES
Large, walnut-shaped, well-spaced, set slightly at a slant. There is no relationship between eye color and coat color (◆).

NECK
Moderately long, thick, and muscular.

BODY
Medium-sized. Round chest. Broad shoulders. Spine as flexible as in other breeds. Moderate to heavy bone and muscle structure.

HEAD
Shaped like an equilateral triangle with rounded contours. Rounded skull. Flat forehead. Cheeks can be broad, particularly in males. Slender muzzle with a slight break (◆). Moderately long nose. Firm but not prominent chin.

EARS
Triangular, moderately broad, straight.

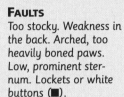

FAULTS
Too stocky. Weakness in the back. Arched, too heavily boned paws. Low, prominent sternum. Lockets or white buttons (■).

LEGS AND PAWS
Short, medium-boned, very muscular. Medium-sized, round, compact paws.

NOTES
Allowable outcross breeds: shorthaired or longhaired cats, while avoiding heavy, massive breeds (■).

TAIL
Moderately thick, tapering to a round tip. Well-furnished, held high and very straight in motion.

COAT
Two varieties:
- shorthaired
- semilonghaired
Silky texture, moderate undercoat. All colors are recognized.

CHARACTERISTICS

While the Munchkin's short legs do not hinder the cat's mobility, they do prevent it from jumping as high as other cats.
Active, lively, and playful, Munchkins are very sociable and affectionate. They adore their owner.
They are easy to groom, especially the shorthaired variety.

(▼) F.I.Fe   (■) L.O.O.F.   (★) C.F.A.   (◆) T.I.C.A.

Ocicat

A spotted athlete with mascara markings around her eyes

"Ocicat" is a combination of the words "ocelot" (a spotted wild cat of the Americas) and "cat." Indeed, this breed has a spotted coat that makes it resemble a small wild cat. In 1964, Virginia Daly, a breeder in Berkeley, Michigan, crossed a Siamese-Abyssinian mix with a chocolate point Siamese in an effort to obtain tabby point Siamese cats. A male in the litter named Tonga and wearing an ivory coat with gold spots was unfortunately neutered. Daly continued her work while other breeders, including Tom Brown, crossed Abyssinians, Siamese, spotted Oriental Shorthairs, Egyptian Maus, and American Shorthairs in order to obtain the Ocicat's current morphology.

The breed was officially recognized by the C.F.A. in 1986, and T.I.C.A. published a standard in 1988. Outcrosses with Abyssinians are now forbidden. In 1989, the first Ocicats were sent to France. Though popular in the United States, the Ocicat is still very rare in Europe.

CINNAMON SPOTTED TABBY

ABOVE AND FACING PAGE: CHOCOLATE SPOTTED TABBY

Ocicat

GENERAL
Large, medium-limbed type, powerful, very muscular, solidly built cat whose spotted coat gives it a wild appearance.
Weight: 2.5 to 6 kg.

CHOCOLATE SILVER SPOTTED TABBY

CINNAMON SPOTTED TABBY

EARS
Moderately large, alert, set at the corners of the head. Lynx tips are appreciated.

EYES
Large, almond-shaped, set slightly at a slant, separated by more than one eye-width. All colors are allowed except blue and are not related to coat color. Colorpoints

HEAD
Slightly triangular, as long as it is wide, with rounded contours. The profile exhibits a slight inward curve. Jowls are tolerated in adult males. Well-defined, broad, slightly angular muzzle. Slight whisker pinch (▼). Slight rise from the bridge of the nose to the brow. Strong chin.

have blue eyes (■). Even, intense color is preferred.

NECK
Arched.

BODY
Large, fairly long, semi-foreign, powerful, but never massive. Fairly deep chest. Well-developed bone and muscle structure.

LEGS AND PAWS
Moderately long, powerful, and muscular. Compact, oval paws.

TAIL
Fairly long, moderately slender, tapering slightly to a dark tip.

COAT
Hair is short but long enough to have several bands of color. Fine, smooth, satiny coat with shiny highlights. Spotted and agouti coat (spotted tabby coat). Each hair, except those at the tip of the tail, has several bands of color.

kings around the eyes and cheeks.

NOTES
Allowable outcross breeds: none.

FAULTS
Massive or stocky body. Blue eyes (▼). Weak and indistinct markings. White spotting or white locket.

The recognized colors are:
- brown (or tawny)
- chocolate
- lilac
- blue
- cinnamon
- fawn

These six colors also exist in silver varieties. All colors must be clear and pleasant. The lightest coloration is normally found on the face, chin, and lower jaw. Markings consist of hairs with darker tipping. They should be clear and distinct. They are darker on the face, legs, and tail than on the body. Dark tail tip. Tabby "M" on the forehead. Mascara mar-

BLUE SILVER SPOTTED TABBY

CINNAMON SPOTTED TABBY

BLACK SILVER SPOTTED TABBY

CHARACTERISTICS
The Ocicat is very lively, highly active, curious, and playful. Despite his similarity to a small wild cat, he is very friendly, gentle, and affectionate. In fact, he will not tolerate solitude. Ocicats are loyal and exclusive like the Siamese, but they have a softer voice. They are very accepting of children but fairly dominant toward other cats. They adapt easily to new living conditions. They are easy to groom, as they simply require regular brushing.

(▼) F.I.Fe   (■) L.O.O.F.   (★) C.F.A.   (◆) T.I.C.A.

Ojos Azules

Extraordinary dark blue eyes

This new breed is descended from Cornflower, a tortie female discovered in New Mexico in 1984. She had very dark blue eyes, a feature normally found only in white or colorpoint cats. The breed's Spanish name means "blue eyes." These cats have blue eyes regardless of coat color. In 1991, T.I.C.A. published a standard. The breed is very rare.

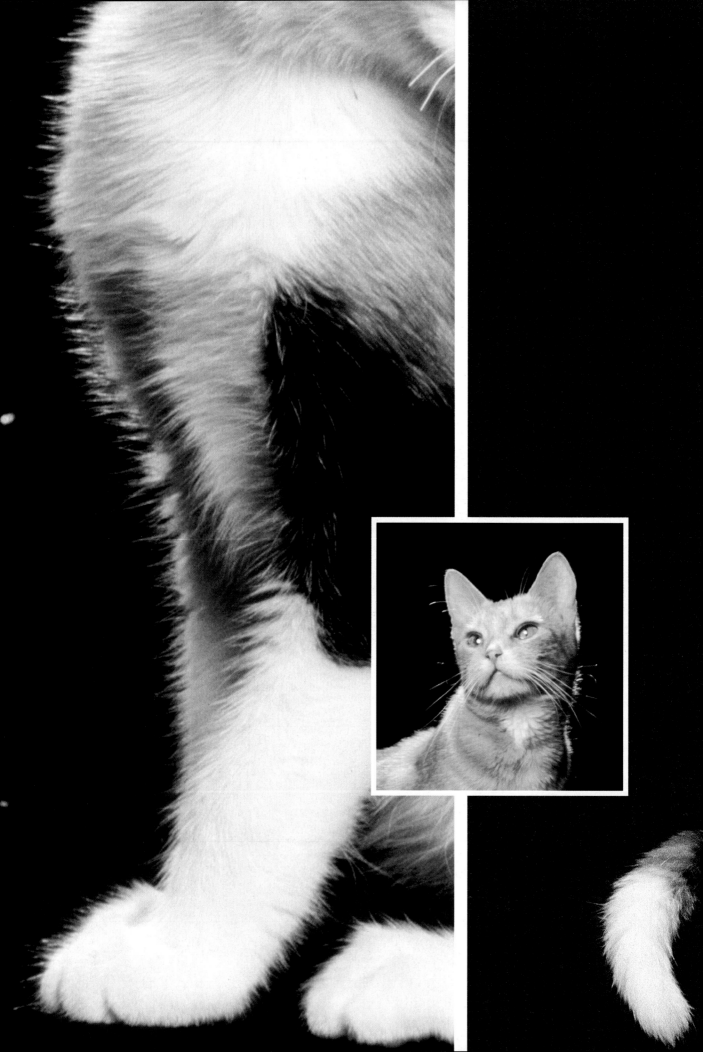

Ojos Azules

GENERAL
Medium-sized.
Type is neither too short nor too long.
Graceful, well-proportioned.

PARTICOLOR

BODY
Neither too long (Oriental type) nor too massive or too short.

LEGS AND PAWS
Hind legs slightly longer than forelegs. Medium to fine-boned. Small paws.

HEAD
Can be inscribed in an equilateral triangle. Slightly rounded forehead. Angular muzzle. Nose with a slight break. Chin is neither prominent nor receding.

EARS
Medium-sized, rounded at the tips, carried fairly high.

EYES
Large, roughly round, but not globular. Light blue or gray-blue in color (neither turquoise nor lavender). In the case of heterochromatic eyes, the center of the eye may be gold, copper, or green. Dark colors are preferred (◆)(■).

NECK
Supple and arched.

TAIL
Proportionate to body, ending in a point.

COAT
Short, fine, soft, silky, shiny hair. Undercoat is not particularly developed but must be dense in color (◆)(■). All colors are allowed. White markings common on most extremities (tip of the tail, muzzle, paws). Spots on the belly or chest are faults. Particolors must have a white tail tip. Ojos Azules with solid white coats are not desirable, as they cannot be distinguished from common white, blue-eyed cats. (◆)(■). Note that white, blue-eyed Ojos Azules are not deaf like most common white, blue-eyed cats. In addition, only white and colorpoint cats can have blue eyes. The Ojos Azules, which always has blue eyes regardless of coat color, is the product of spontaneous mutation by a dominant gene.

NOTES
Allowable outcross breeds: none.

FAULTS
Too large. Too svelte or too massive. Pointed muzzle. Pale, small, Oriental eyes. Coat too downy, too fluffy. Distinct spots on the chest and belly. Disqualify: eyes not blue. Particolors with a tail tip other than white.

CHARACTERISTICS
This cat is active, friendly, affectionate, and easy to groom.

(▼)F.I.Fe   (■) L.O.O.F.   (★) C.F.A.   (◆) T.I.C.A.

Oriental Shorthair

The Greyhound of cats

Both originally from Thailand, the Oriental Shorthair and the Siamese differ only in coat and eye color. Some believe the Oriental Shorthair is the original type, while the Siamese, a colorpoint Oriental Shorthair, is a variety.

Both breeds arrived in Great Britain in the late 19th century. From 1920 to 1930, the Siamese was more popular than the Oriental Shorthair, which did not interest breeders until after 1950.

By crossing Siamese and European Shorthairs of different colors, breeders successively obtained chocolate, white (Foreign White), and blue Oriental Shorthairs.

By 1968, American breeders began breeding programs focused on an extreme morphological type closely resembling today's Siamese, while the British preferred a moderate type. The C.F.A. recognized the breed in 1972 as the Oriental Shorthair. In 1994 it approved the Oriental Longhair, or Mandarin. The Oriental Shorthair is not very common.

Oriental Shorthair

GENERAL
Medium-sized, long-limbed, svelte, elegant but muscular. Long limbs. Short hair. Weight: 4 to 6.5 kg.

HEAD
Long, can be inscribed in an isosceles triangle. Straight profile without stop. The skull, seen in profile, is slightly convex. Slender, well-formed muzzle. Long, straight nose. Medium-sized chin.

EARS
Large, well-spaced, broad at the base, pointed.

EYES
Medium-sized, almond-shaped, set at a pronounced slant.

Separated by one eye-width. Emerald green or jade except in the white Oriental Shorthair, which has blue eyes. Yellow or copper eyes are accepted for red and cream coats (◆)(▼). Note that the color may not be acquired until the cat is one year old.

COAT
Hair is short, dense, fine, silky, lying flat.

FOUR MAIN GROUPS OF VARIETIES:

- Solid coats: solid color without stripes or tabby markings. Pure white, ebony, blue, chocolate, lilac, cinnamon, fawn.

TORTOISESHELL

NECK
Long, slender.

BODY
Long, svelte, slender, tubular. Narrow abdomen. Fine-boned. Firm, long muscles.

LEGS AND PAWS
Long, slender, proportionate to the body. Forelegs slightly shorter than hind legs. Fine-boned. Small, oval paws.

TAIL
Long and slender, even at the base, tapering to a point.

- Tortoiseshell coats and variants: orange, black, and chocolate.
- Coats in which the base of the hair is diluted:
- Smoke: dilute color in a short band at the base.
- Silver: pigmentation at the hair tip (tipping).
- Tabby coats:
- Blotched: broad stripes.
- Mackerel: narrow stripes perpendicular to the spine.
- Spotted: circular, evenly distributed spots.

The spotted tabby Oriental Shorthair, also called Maus, is often

mistaken for the Egyptian Mau. Between stripes and spots, agouti-type hairs with alternating dark and light bands.

CONDITION
Very muscular, firm, but not emaciated. Neither underweight or heavy (◆)

NOTES
Allowable outcross breeds: Siamese, Balinese, Oriental Longhair.

FAULTS
Round, broad, excessively short head. Muzzle too short, too broad. Presence of a stop or whisker pinch. Receding or massive chin. Ears too small, too close together. Round, small eyes. Short, massive body. Short legs. Heavy-boned. Rough coat.

CHARACTERISTICS
Like the Siamese, Oriental Shorthairs are very lively, extraverted, proud, and captivating. They are sociable and do not like being alone. These playful cats can tolerate children. They are affectionate and often very possessive, even tyrannical, toward their owner. Indifference is not acceptable to them. They are "talkative" and have a loud voice.
They have the temperament of a hunter.
Female cats are sexually precocious (entering puberty by 9 months) and have frequent heats. They are more prolific than average for domestic cats. They are easy to groom, as weekly.

(▼) F.I.Fe　　(■) L.O.O.F.　　(★) C.F.A.　　(◆) T.I.C.A.

Ragdoll

Country of Origin: United States

Big and floppy, like a ragdoll

Around 1960 in Riverside, east of Los Angeles, a white Turkish Angora type female named Josephine was born in the home of Ms. Pennels. This cat was crossed with a gloved Birman type tom named Daddy Warbucks. Their litter sparked the interest of Ann Baker, who set about intense inbreeding. Thus was created the so-called Ragdoll breed, named for the way the cats typically relax completely, with low muscle tone.

The Ragdoll was approved in the United States in 1965. In 1971, Baker founded the International Ragdoll Cat Association (I.R.C.A.).

In 1969, two Ragdolls from Baker's cattery were sent to Great Britain. A British Ragdoll club was founded in 1987.

The G.C.C.G. recognized the breed in 1991, and the F.I.Fe. recognized it in 1992.

The Ragdoll arrived in Germany and France in 1985 and 1986, respectively. In 1993, a French breed club was created.

The Ragdoll is quite uncommon outside the United States.

Ragdoll

GENERAL
Large, solid, muscular, powerful.
Weight: 4.5 to 9 kg.

HEAD
Medium-sized, broad, slightly wedge-shaped with rounded contours. Skull is flat between the ears. Slightly rounded forehead. Well-developed cheeks. Rounded, moderately long, well-developed muzzle. Nose with gentle break. Well-developed chin.

EARS
Medium-sized, broad at the base, well-spaced, pointed slightly forward, rounded at the tips.

EYES
Large, oval, slightly slanted. As intense a shade of blue as possible, corresponding to coat color.

NECK
Short and strong.

BODY
Large, long, well-built. Broad, well-developed chest. Heavy, solid hindquarters. Medium-boned.

LEGS AND PAWS
Moderately long, medium-boned. Hind legs slightly longer than forelegs. Large, round, compact paws with tufts of hair between the toes.

TAIL
Long, proportionate to the body, fairly thick at the base, tapering slightly to the tip. Well-furnished and fluffy.

COAT
Semilong, soft, silky hair lying flat against the body. In motion, the hair separates into tufts. Very substantial ruff.
Four classic colors (seal, blue, chocolate, lilac). Three patterns for coats with points:
- Colorpoint: body lighter in color than extremities (points).
- Mitted or gloved: also with Siamese pattern, but with gloves on the paws. White blaze on the nose. White chin.
- Bicolor: colorpoint with white extending over the face in an inverted V; four white paws. White chest and belly.
Coloring is not complete until the cat is two years old and darkens with age.

NOTES
Allowable outcross breeds: none.

FAULTS
Narrow head. Nose with a stop (▼). Large or small, pointed ears. Almond-shaped eyes (▼). Neck too long or too slender. Stocky body. Narrow chest. Short legs. Lack of interdigital hair. Short tail. Short hair. Disqualify: white markings in the colorpoint; absence of white chin in the mitted; dark markings on the white mask in the bicolor. Eyes of a color other than blue (▼).

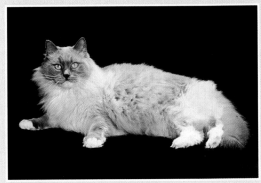

CHARACTERISTICS
The Ragdoll's calmness and his debonair, docile temperament make him a very pleasant companion. He does not tolerate agitation and noise. Ragdolls are sociable, getting along well with other cats and with dogs. Very affectionate and loving, they like company and despise solitude. They adapt very well to apartment life. They are not noisy.
They do not reach full size until the age of three or four. In terms of grooming, they require frequent brushing and combing.

(▼) F.I.Fe.   (■) L.O.O.F.   (★) C.F.A.   (◆) T.I.C.A.

Birman

Very impressive, with dark blue eyes and white gloves

Having appeared recently in Europe, this cat's origins are still mysterious. British travelers are thought to have brought back a pair of cats from the so-called Lao-tsun Temple in Burma. A certain Ms. Leotardi in southern France owned Poupée de Madalpour, a seal point Birman shown in Paris in 1926. This cat's parents, from Burma, were given to Leotardi by a certain Ms. Thadde-Haddish.

Actually, the first specimens resulted from a cross between a Siamese with white markings on the paws and a longhaired cat (Angora or Persian) made in the 1920s in the region of Nice, in France. By around 1930, a male seal point named Dieu d'Arakan was the star of the shows.
The breed nearly disappeared during World War II. After the war, colorpoint Persian blood was added to limit inbreeding. In 1950, the breed was named Chat Sacré de Birmanie (Birman in English) in order to avoid any confusion with "Burmese", the adjective form of the word Burma.

Introduced to the United States in 1959-1960 and to Great Britain in 1965, where it was officially recognized, this highly prized breed has become very popular.

Birman

GENERAL
Medium-sized, medium-limbed type but imposing and massive.
Weight: 4.5 to 8 kg.
Longhaired

EARS
Medium-sized with rounded tips, moderately spaced to well-spaced. Slightly slanted. Well-furnished on the inside surface.

EYES
Large, nearly round, well-spaced. Color: blue, as dark as possible.

HEAD
Large, broad, fairly round. Slightly longer than it is wide. Fairly rounded skull. Slightly domed forehead. Full cheeks, high, prominent cheekbones. Roman nose of medium length with a defined (◆) or absent (▼) stop. Well-developed muzzle. Strong. Firm chin.

TAIL
Moderately long, carried erect. Plume.

COAT
Silky hair, semilong to long on the ruff, body, flanks, and tail. Short on the face and limbs. Sparse undercoat. Coat pigmented only on the extremities or points (mask, ears, paws, and tail), as in the Siamese.

2/3 the distance between the large paw pad and the hock.
The darker markings can be seal point (dark brown), chocolate point (light brown), blue point (gray-blue), lilac point (pinkish steel gray), red point (reddish-brown), or cream point.
The rest of the coat varies from white to cream. The paw pads are pink or pink with spots of color.
Kittens are born almost entirely white. The points and gloves do not appear until around 1-2 months. The color of the body and markings is not final until adulthood. In addition, the coat darkens with age.

NOTES
Allowable outcross breeds: none.

FAULTS
White or colored markings on the chest or belly. Disqualify: a non-gloved toe. White on the points.

NECK
Medium-sized, muscular.

BODY
Fairly long, fairly heavy (semi-cobby). Strong boned; powerful, firm muscles.

LEGS AND PAWS
Moderately long, strong. Heavy-boned, muscular. Round, firm paws. Tufts of fur between the toes.

A good contrast between the color of the points and the rest of the body is required. White markings, or gloves, on the paws. These absolutely pure white gloves must stop at the joint or transition between the toes and the metacarpus, which they should not go past. On the plantar surface of the hind paws, the gloves end in a point (gauntlets) at 1/2 to

CHARACTERISTICS

Halfway between the Persian and the Siamese, the Birman is calm, well-balanced, and neither passive nor exuberant. He is friendly toward other cats and toward dogs.
Playful Birmans are good companions for children, but they also like peace and quiet. Gentle, affectionate (especially males), and often somewhat possessive, Birmans do not tolerate indifference and are even less fond of solitude. They have a soft voice. Outside, they are hardy and athletic, making excellent hunters.
They require daily brushing during the shedding season. Otherwise, weekly brushing and combing are enough.

(▼) F.I.Fe.   (■) L.O.O.F.   (★) C.F.A.   (◆) T.I.C.A.

Scottish Fold

Country of Origin: Scotland

A roly-poly guy with little ears set in a caplike fashion, flat against the head

In his 1897 Treatise on Animal Breeding, Professor Cornevin indicated a breed of shorthaired cat with pendulous ears that was fattened for eating in its native China. A spontaneous mutation by a dominant gene that caused the ear flap to fold forward was first observed in Scotland in 1961. William Ross, a shepherd in Tayside, and his wife Mary noticed a white female cat named Susie with folded ears who lived at the McRae family's neighboring farm. Susie gave birth to Snooks, a white female with the same type of ears. When crossed with a British Shorthair, she gave birth to a white male named Snowball. This new breed was named after the "folded ear" mutation. Unfortunately, limb, tail, and joint deformities linked to the dominant Fd gene appeared, to such an extent that the G.C.C.F. discontinued registration of the breed in 1973.

In 1971, Mary Ross sent some Scottish Folds to Neil Todd, an American geneticist in Massachusetts who set about breeding the cats again. Crosses were made with British Shorthairs, Exotic Shorthairs, and American Shorthairs in order to prevent severe joint disorders.
The C.F.A. and then T.I.C.A. recognized the breed, which was highly successful in the United States. A return to Europe began in 1980, with the first Scottish Fold born in France in 1982. Recognized neither by the F.I.Fe. nor the G.C.C.F., the Scottish Fold is relatively rare throughout Europe.

In the United States, a Scottish Fold was crossed with a Persian to produce a new, longhaired version called the Highland Fold or Longhaired Scottish Fold, which is recognized by T.I.C.A.

A cross with rexes made in Germany in 1987 gave rise to the Pudelkatze or Poodle Cat, a curly-coated feline with pendulous ears. With a very limited population, the Pudelkatze is not yet recognized as a new breed.

Scottish Fold

GENERAL
Short-limbed type, stout, stocky, entirely round in form.
Weight: 2.5 to 6 kg.

NECK
Short and muscular.

BODY
Medium-sized, stout, rounded, very muscular. Medium-boned.

LEGS AND PAWS
Length in proportion to the body. Medium-boned. Round, compact paws.

COAT
Two varieties:
- short, thick, tight, very dense, fluffy, resilient coat
- semilong: this variety is called the Highland Fold.
All colors are recognized. Chocolate, lilac, and Siamese markings are not allowed (*).

HEAD
Round. Domed forehead. Rounded cheeks. Jowls allowed in adult males. Broad, short nose. Slight stop accepted. Well-rounded muzzle. Round whisker pad. Firm chin.

FAULTS
Head too slender, pointed. Stop too pronounced. Disqualify: tail too short, lacking flexibility due to abnormally thick vertebrae.

EARS
Small, folded forward in a caplike fashion. Well-spaced, rounded at the tips.

EYES
Large, round, fairly well-spaced. The color corresponds to that of the coat.

TAIL
No longer than 2/3 the length of the body. Thick at the base, tapering to a rounded tip. Very supple and flexible.

NOTES
Allowable outcross breeds: British Shorthair (■), Exotic Shorthair, American Shorthair (*).

CHARACTERISTICS
Scottish Folds are especially peaceful, non-dominant, and friendly toward other cats and toward dogs. Gentle, very affectionate, loving, and very playful, they adore family life. They are discrete and have a soft voice.
Hardy and resistant, these cats are excellent hunters. In terms of grooming, they require weekly brushing. During shedding, their fluffy coat must be combed regularly. It is best to keep an eye on their ears. In order to prevent bone deformities, two cats with folded ears should not be mated together. Instead, the Scottish Fold is crossed with prick-eared cats like the British Shorthair or American Shorthair.
The "folded ear" characteristic is not visible until the third or fourth week, and the degree of folding cannot be observed until the fifth or sixth week.

(▼) F.I.Fe   (■) L.O.O.F.   (★) C.F.A.   (◆) T.I.C.A.

Selkirk Rex

Country of Origin:
United States
Other Name:
Selkirk Rex Longhair,
Sheep Cat

Curly-coated like a Poodle or sheep

In 1987 in Wyoming, a cross between a flat-coated female and a curly-coated male produced a curly-coated female named Miss DePesto of NoFace, who was adopted by Jeri Newman, a breeder of Persians in Montana. In 1988, Miss DePesto was crossed with Photo Finish, a black Persian, and gave birth to three curly-coated kittens. Later bred to one of her kittens, she again produced three curly-coated offspring. Jeri Newman named this new breed after the nearby Selkirk Mountains.

This spontaneous mutation is caused by a new dominant gene different from other curly-coated genes.

While the Devon Rex resembles E.T., the Selkirk Rex looks more like a Poodle. Popular in the United States, the Selkirk Rex appeared in Europe in 1990 and is still rare.

Selkirk Rex

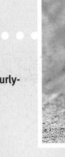

GENERAL
Medium-sized, the largest and shaggiest of the curly-coated feline breeds.
Heavy-boned.
Weight: 3 to 5 kg.

EARS
Medium-sized, well-spaced, ending in slightly rounded tips. Curly hair on the inside.

EYES
Large, round, well-spaced. Even color corresponding to that of the coat.

HEAD
Medium-sized, round, and broad. Skull with a gentle curve. Round forehead. Full cheeks in both sexes. Short, angular muzzle. Hooked nose, slight stop. Curly whiskers and eyebrows. Heavy jaws.

condition, especially in females. Kittens are born curly-coated. The curls relax and reform around 8-10 months. The coat continues to develop until the age of two. Shorthaired and longhaired varieties. All colors are recognized (■), with clearly defined shades being preferred. White lockets are allowed (◆).

BODY
Moderately long, rectangular, stout, heavy. Muscular and strong boned.

NOTES
Allowable outcross breeds: none.

FAULTS
Disqualify: break in the nose. Crossed eyes. Kink in the tail (■).

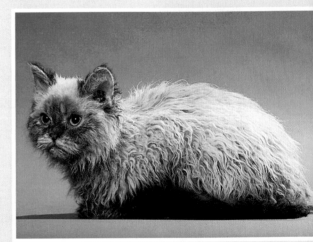

NECK
Short, thick.

LEGS AND PAWS
Moderately long. Medium to strong bone and muscle structure. Large, round paws.

TAIL
Moderately long, thick, with a rounded tip.

COAT
Thick coat with well-separated curls that are especially numerous on the neck and tail and cover the entire body. No hairless areas. Thick undercoat.
The curliness of the coat varies with the climate, seasons, and hormonal

CHARACTERISTICS
This active cat with a debonair, calm character gets along well with other cats and with dogs.
The playful Selkirk Rex is an excellent companion for children.
Gentle and affectionate, Selkirks are very pleasant to live with. They adapt well to apartment life.
They need minimal grooming. Light brushing twice a month is enough. They should be bathed several days before a show.

(▼) F.I.Fe   (■) L.O.O.F.   (★) C.F.A.   (◆) T.I.C.A.

48

Siberian Cat

Countries of origin:
Russia, Ukraine
Original Name:
Sibirskaya Koshka
Other Name: Sibi

His pedigree must indicate his Russian origin

This large cat lived in the wilds of Russia for quite a while. It might be the product of crosses between domestic cats brought to Siberia and the Ukraine and local wild cats. Its thick, insulating fur is adapted to its harsh native climate.

Mussa, a female red and white tabby, and Tima, a tom, were purchased in St. Petersburg and brought to Berlin in 1987. Hans and Betti Schulz bred the first Siberians in their Newski Cattery. In 1990, some fifteen specimens were recorded in western Europe.

The Siberian has been established in France since 1991. It was recognized by the F.I.Fe. in 1997.

In 1990, Elizabeth Terrell imported the first specimens of the breed to her Starpoint Cattery in the United States. T.I.C.A. recognized the Siberian and published a standard in 1998.

The breed is quite uncommon outside eastern Europe and the United States.

Siberian Cat

GENERAL
Very large, compact, massive, heavy. Powerful, pronounced muscle structure.
Weight: 4.5 to 9 kg.
Stockier than the Maine Coon; head more rounded than that of the Norwegian Forest Cat.

HEAD
Medium-sized, broad, triangular, with rounded contours. Flat top of the head. Slightly curved forehead. Cheeks not pronounced or prominent. Rounded, moderately long muzzle. Nose broad between the eyes, receding toward the tip, with a slight curve. Round chin. Long, thick whiskers (■).

EARS
Moderately broad, rounded tips. Short hair on the backs of the ears, long on the inside. Lynx tips desirable.

EYES
Large, nearly round, well-spaced, set at a slight slant. Traditional adult color: green to yellow, but blue in colorpoints. No relationship to coat color (◆).

NECK
Moderately long, rounded, thick, very muscular.

BODY
Compact, moderately long. Long back, slightly curved or arched. Well-rounded chest.

Strong bone and muscle structure.

LEGS AND PAWS
Hind legs slightly longer than forelegs. Heavy-boned, very muscular. Large, round paws with tufts of hair between the toes. All claws but one are retractile (■).

TAIL
Moderately long, broad at the base, well-furnished, and thick.

COAT
Semilong to long hair, fluffy, oily, waterproof, effectively protecting the cat from bitter cold. Stiff guard hairs. Long hair on the belly, slightly shorter on the shoulders and part of the chest. Long, well-furnished ruff. Thick undercoat. All traditional colors and color combinations are accepted except chocolate and lilac. Colorpoint specimens are known as Neva Mascarade (■).

NOTES
Allowable outcross breeds: none.

FAULTS
Straight profile. Narrow or pointed muzzle. Almond-shaped eyes. Very long legs. Disqualify: stop on the nose (■).

 CHARACTERISTICS
These large cats exude quiet strength. They are quite lively and can be highly active. Despite a strong personality and character, Siberians are very friendly toward other cats. They are playful and get along well with children. They are affectionate and very attached to their owner. They have a soft voice. These hardy, water-loving cats are good climbers and excellent jumpers. They need space for their emotional well-being, and their beautiful coat makes them well-adapted to outdoor life.
They are not fully grown until the age of five.
They are easy to groom, since their coat resists matting. Normally, weekly brushing is enough. During heavy shedding in the spring, daily brushing is required.

(▼) F.I.Fe   (■) L.O.O.F.   (★) C.F.A.   (◆) T.I.C.A.

Singapura

Country of Origin: Singapore Island

The lightest of the domestic cats

"Singapura" is the Malaysian name for Singapore Island and also designates a true common cat who walks the streets of the capital. American tourists Tommy and Hal Meadows noticed the cats in 1974. The following year, they became the first to import the breed to California. They acquired three cats (Tess, Tickle, and Puss) who were being shown by 1976. T. and S. Svenson were among the ardent supporters of the breed. In 1980, more Singapuras were brought to the United States. T.I.C.A. and then the C.F.A. recognized them in 1984 and 1988, respectively. The first specimens of the breed were reported in France and Great Britain around 1988-1989. The F.I.Fe. has not yet recognized it. Although the Singapura was developed in the United States, it is not common there. It is rare in France.

Singapura

GENERAL
Compact cat, small to medium in size.
Weight: under 3 kg (the lightest of the domestic cats).
Ticked coat.

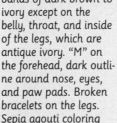

COAT
Fine, very short hair, not fluffy, lying flat against the body. Ticking of four or more alternating on a warm antique ivory background (brown ticked tabby). Dark salmon pink nose, pinkish-brown paw

NOTES
Allowable outcross breeds: none.

FAULTS
Small ears and eyes. Muzzle too short. Fluffy coat. Cold, grayish cast. Absence of bars on the inside of the legs. Absence of necklaces and outline around the nose. Disqualify: blue eyes. Continuous necklaces, circular bracelets on legs, bars on tail. White lockets or any other markings.

HEAD
Small, round. Jowls allowed in adult males. Short, broad muzzle. Delicately domed nose with a slight stop below the line of the eyes. Well-developed, rounded chin. Well-defined whisker pads.

EARS
Large, slightly pointed, broad at the base, moderately spaced. Shiny, richly colored coat.

EYES
Large, almond-shaped, accentuated by dark outlines. Separated by one eye-width. Color: green, gold, or copper. Blue is not allowed.

NECK
Short and thick.

BODY
Small to medium-sized, moderately stocky, compact. Well-built, muscular. Rounded rib cage, slightly arched back, round croup.

LEGS AND PAWS
Muscular, fine-boned legs. Small, oval paws.

TAIL
Moderately long, fairly thin but not excessively tapered. Rounded tip.

bands of dark brown to ivory except on the belly, throat, and inside of the legs, which are antique ivory. "M" on the forehead, dark outline around nose, eyes, and paw pads. Broken bracelets on the legs. Sepia agouti coloring with dark brown ticking pads. The inside of the ears is salmon-colored with ivory hair. Hair along the spine and on the tail tip may be dark.

CHARACTERISTICS
The Singapura is well-balanced. Into everything, sociable, very affectionate, and loving, these cats are sensitive and demand petting. They are discreet and have a very soft voice. They follow their owner everywhere.
Outside, they are excellent hunters.
Female Singapuras are known for being very loving mothers. In terms of grooming, they require weekly brushing.

(▼) F.I.Fe   (■) L.O.OF.   (★) C.F.A.   (◆) T.I.C.A.

56

Snowshoe

Country of Origin: United States

A white-footed breed made in America

This new breed resulted from a desire to combine into one cat the points of the Siamese and the gloved paws of the Birman. It was created in the United States in the 1960s by Dorothy Hinds-Daugherty, a breeder in Philadelphia, by crossing the Siamese with the bicolor American Shorthair. The Snowshoe looks like a hefty Siamese sporting white gloves.

Recognized by T.I.C.A. in the 1980s, the breed has been somewhat successful in the United States but remains rare.

Snowshoe

GENERAL
Medium-sized.
Weight: 2.5 to 5.5 kg.
A combination of strength, grace, and elegance.
It is larger and heavier than the Siamese.

EARS
Medium to large in size, broad at the base, slightly rounded at the tips. Sparsely furnished.

HEAD
Medium-sized, shaped almost like an equilateral triangle (◆), with slightly rounded contours. Slightly flat forehead. High cheekbones. Fairly broad muzzle, neither too broad nor pointed or angular. No whisker pinch (◆). Straight nose with very slight curve at the base of the forehead. Firm chin.

Legs and paws
Proportionate to the body. Medium bone and muscle structure. Medium-sized, oval paws.

EYES
Fairly large, oval, walnut-shaped, slightly slanted. Separated by one eye-width. Color: blue, as intense as possible.

NECK
Moderately long.

BODY
Well-balanced, semi-foreign, can be inscribed in a rectangle. Croup slightly higher than shoulders. Slightly arched back. Medium-boned. Muscles powerful but not massive.

TAIL
Length in proportion to the body. Moderately thick at the base, tapering slightly to the tip.

COAT
Short, thick, shiny hair lying flat against the body. Very slight undercoat. Classic Siamese colors: seal, blue, chocolate, and lilac.
The color of the extremities (points) should contrast clearly with the body color, which is always lighter. The eyes are always blue.
Inverted V on the forehead, white markings on the paws. Ideally, four even gloves. The nose leather may be white with no coloring, flesh colored, or multi-colored.
In the mitted variety, the white should cover no more than 1/3 the body. In the bicolor, the white should cover no more than 2/3 the body. Among the recognized varieties are:
- seal point: dark buff coat on the back, light buff on the belly and chest with brown points
- blue point: bluish-white body, with a lighter belly and chest. The points are dark bluish-gray.
Snowshoes are born all white, and the points darken with age.

NOTES
Allowable outcross breeds: none.

FAULTS
Head too long. Muzzle too broad. Small, rounded ears. Small, rounded, very slanted eyes. Body very long and frail or too short and massive. Thin tail. Knotted, fine-boned legs. Disqualify: longhaired coat, eyes not blue. White markings covering the colored points. Fewer than four white "shoes" (■).

CHARACTERISTICS
This extremely lively cat with a strong personality is a good hunter. He is sociable and gets along well with other cats and with dogs.
Playful Snowshoes are excellent companions for children.
They are gentle and very affectionate toward their owner. Less demanding than the Siamese, they are more talkative than the American Shorthair. In terms of grooming, they require weekly brushing.

(▼) F.I.Fe   (■) L.O.O.F.   (★) C.F.A.   (◆) T.I.C.A.

African Shorthair

Country of Origin: Kenya (Africa)
Original Name: Khadzonzo
Other Name: Sokoke

From the trees of Kenya

Khadzonzos have long inhabited the forests of Kenya's Sokoke district. Spending their time in trees, they are voracious insect hunters. In the 1970s, Jeni Slater, an Englishwoman living in Kenya, adopted a female cat and her kittens, the origin of the breed. Canadian native Gloria Moldrup, a friend of Slater, first brought two kittens back to Denmark, then began importing them regularly around 1980. All her cats came from Jeni Slater's cattery. Moldrup started a breeding program with other breeders.

In 1983, the breed was named the African Shorthair. It was officially recognized first in Denmark in 1992, then in other countries. The F.I.Fe. approved it in 1993. Internationally, it received the name Sokoke. It is still extremely rare.

African Shorthair

GENERAL
Medium-sized, svelte, with a marbled tabby coat.

HEAD
Appears small compared to body. Wedge-shaped. Nearly flat top of the skull. High, well-defined cheekbones. Nose moderately long, with a gentle concave curve. Strong, broad chin. Well-defined whisker pads. No whisker pinch.

EARS
Medium-sized, broad at the base, slightly rounded tips. Moderately spaced. Lynx tips desirable.

EYES
Large, slightly almond-shaped, moderately spaced, slightly slanted toward the nose. Amber to light green. Outlined in the same color as the solid parts of the markings.

BODY
Moderately long, svelte, very muscular. Solidly boned. Well-developed chest.

LEGS AND PAWS
Long, svelte, and very muscular. Forelegs are shorter than hind legs. Oval paws.

TAIL
Moderately long, thick at the base, tapering to the tip.

COAT
Short hair, shiny but not silky, lying flat against the body. Little or no undercoat. Recognized color: brown blotched tabby, that is, brown or black marbled tabby with a somewhat darker base. The tip of the tail is always black. Each hair has alternating light and dark bands.

NOTES
Allowable outcross breeds: none.

FAULTS
Head too Oriental in type. Stop too pronounced. Whisker pinch. Body too stocky and lacking elegance. Disqualify: white locket or white markings anywhere on the body except the nostrils, chin, and throat.

CHARACTERISTICS
This active, lively, independent cat is a very good climber and swimmer.
He is sociable with other cats and with dogs. Gentle and affectionate, he makes a good companion.
He can adapt to apartment life, but he needs space and therefore appreciates a yard.
Weekly brushing is enough to maintain his coat.

(▼) F.I.Fe   (■) L.O.O.F.   (★) C.F.A.   (◆) T.I.C.A.

Somali

Countries of origin: United States, Canada
Other Name: Longhaired Abyssinian

A fox in the house

For a long time, kittens with semilong, soft hair appeared in litters of Abyssinians (which were actually of a much heavier type than today). But breeders were not interested in them and did not use them in reproduction. The gene responsible for semilong hair was probably introduced by crossing Abyssinians with longhaired cats (Persians or Angoras).

In Canada, it was not until the 1960s that breeders Don Richings and Mary Mailing and judge Ken MacGill became interested in these new cats. In 1967, American breeder Evelyn Mague managed to pin down the semilonghair gene in Abyssinians. The new breed was named the Somali, in reference to the neighboring country of Ethiopia, the supposed birthplace of the Abyssinian.

Mague founded the Lynn Lee Cattery and the first breed club in the United States. She showed the first Somali in 1972. The C.F.A. recognized the breed in 1978.

Lynn Lee's Picasso and Lynn Lee's Pearl, two Somalis from Mague's cattery, arrived in France in 1979.

The F.I.Fe. approved the breed in 1982. It is highly prized by more and more people.

Somali

GENERAL
Medium in size and "royal" in appearance, the Somali resembles an Abyssinian but has semilong hair. Long-limbed type.
Weight: 3.5 to 5.5 kg.

HEAD
Viewed from the front, shaped like a triangle with rounded contours. Slightly domed forehead. In profile, the head has a gentle curve. Muzzle neither small nor pointed. A whisker pinch is a fault (▼). Nose of medium length, without stop. Firm, well-developed chin.

EARS
Large, broad at the base, fairly well-spaced, with slightly rounded tips. A "thumbprint" is desirable on the back of the ear. Lynx tips are appreciated.

EYES
Large, almond-shaped, well-spaced, with dark markings below the eyes. Above each eye is a short vertical marking (remnants of the tabby "M"). Color: amber, green, gold.

NECK
Carried gracefully.

BODY
Medium in size and length, semi-foreign

type, graceful. Slightly arched back. Powerful muscles.

LEGS AND PAWS
Long and thin, well-muscled. Compact, oval paws. The Somali appears to stand on tiptoe.

TAIL
Long, carried high, and well-furnished like that of a fox.

COAT
Semilong, dense, very fine, and soft hair. Short on the face, front of the legs, and shoulders; semilong on the back,

flanks, chest, and belly. It is long on the throat (ruff), behind the thighs (britches), and tail (plume). The undercoat is not long as in the Persian.

Color: Ticked coat, that is, the presence on each hair of alternating bands of dark and light coloration. At least two or three bands, up to eight banks. The tip of the hair must have a

dark band. Let us mention several varieties:
- ruddy ("usual" in Great Britain): black bands and apricot bands

- blue: slate blue bands and cream bands
- red (or sorrel): chocolate bands and apricot bands
- fawn beige: dark cream bands and dull beige bands
- black silver: black bands and white bands
- sorrel silver: chocolate bands and white bands
- blue silver: blue bands and white bands
The C.F.A. accepts the ruddy, red, blue, and fawn. A greater number of colors is accepted in Europe.

NOTES
Allowable outcross breeds: Abyssinian.

FAULTS
Round, Siamese type head. Pronounced stop. Round eyes without markings the same color as ticking. Small or pointed ears. Body too stocky. Short legs and tail. Disqualify: absence of or too little ticking. Ringed tail and legs. Whip tail. White locket, markings on the belly, etc.

 CHARACTERISTICS
This very lively cat is active but not exuberant. Hardy, well-balanced, and even-tempered, he is calmer than the Abyssinian.
Somalis have a gentle temperament and are sociable toward other cats and strangers. Very playful, they get along well with children. Gentle and very affectionate, they demand lots of attention but are less possessive than the Abyssinian.
Although a bit sensitive to cold, they do not tolerate apartment life very well. They are big hunters, so a yard suits them.
In terms of grooming, they require only weekly brushing. During shedding, they should be brushed daily.
Somali kittens are born with nearly bicolor coats: dark on the back and light on the underparts. Ticking appears very gradually. Similarly, the length and final appearance of the coat are not attained until the second year.

(▼)F.I.Fe　(■) L.O.O.F.　(★) C.F.A.　(◆) T.I.C.A.

Sphynx

A hairless cat highly sensitive to sunlight

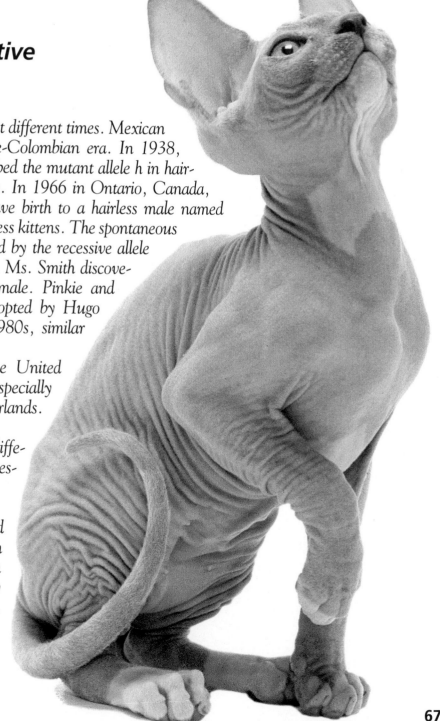

Hairless cats appeared in the world at different times. Mexican hairless cats date back to the pre-Colombian era. In 1938, French professor E. Letard described the mutant allele h in hairless kittens produced by a pair of Siamese. In 1966 in Ontario, Canada, Ms. Micalwaith's female cat Elisabeth gave birth to a hairless male named Prune. Prune and Elisabeth produced hairless kittens. The spontaneous mutation responsible for this trait is caused by the recessive allele hr. Also in Ontario and at the same time, Ms. Smith discovered Bambi, a black and white hairless male. Pinkie and Squeakie, two hairless females, were adopted by Hugo Hernandez in the Netherlands. In the 1980s, similar cases were reported in Great Britain.

As interest in these cats declined in the United States, their popularity grew in Europe, especially in France by 1983, as well as in the Netherlands.

It is true that it is impossible to remain indifferent to these cats, adored by some and detested by others.

Seeing the success of these cats in shows and the curiosity they generated, American breeders began importing Sphynxes from Europe. The breed is recognized by T.I.C.A., but the C.F.A. and the F.I.Fe. have rejected it. The Sphynx is quite rare.

67

Sphynx

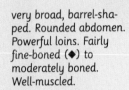

GENERAL
Medium-sized.
Weight: 3.5 to 7 kg.
Medium-boned, fairly muscular.
Skin covered with a fine down.
Sparse hairs. Wrinkled skin.

EARS
Very large, very broad at the base. The inside is totally hairless. Light down on the back of the ear is allowed

EYES
Large, lemon-shaped, upper corner pointing toward ears, well-spaced. Color corresponding to that of the coat.

HEAD
Medium-sized, angular, slightly triangular. Longer than it is wide. Flat forehead. Prominent cheek bones. Short nose, pronounced (■) or slight (◆) stop. Muzzle very rounded, broad, short. Pronounced whisker pinch. Firm chin. Whiskers sparse, short, or absent.

very broad, barrel-shaped. Rounded abdomen. Powerful loins. Fairly fine-boned (◆) to moderately boned. Well-muscled.

LEGS AND PAWS
Length proportional to that of the body. Forelegs slightly arched, slightly shorter than hind legs.

TAIL
Moderately long, slender, whip tail known as a "rat tail." It may have a tuft of hair on the tip ("lion tail").

COAT
Skin appears hairless and resembles that of a chamois in texture. Skin wrinkled on the head, body, and legs. Elsewhere, it is taut. The coat is limited to a fine down covering most of the body. A few hairs are present on the face, paws, tail, and testicles. Thus, "hairless cat" is a misnomer. All colors are recognized, as are all patterns. White looks pinkish, and black looks dark gray.

NOTES
Allowable outcross breeds: none.

FAULTS
Too frail, delicate in appearance. Too small in size. Head too narrow. Straight profile. Compact or long body. Disqualify: eyes too small. Absence of whisker pinch. Toes too small (◆). Kinky hair of Devon Rex or Cornish Rex during shedding. Obvious tweezing or shaving.

NECK
Long, arched, muscular, powerful in males.

BODY
Medium-sized. Chest

Medium-boned. Firm, well-developed muscles. Medium-sized, oval paws with long toes. Very thick paw pads.

CHARACTERISTICS
The Sphynx is lively, mischievous, playful, and independent. Friendly toward other cats and toward dogs, Sphynxes are never aggressive. Very affectionate and even possessive, they adore being doted on.
Apartment life is perfect for them, since they are sensitive to cold, heat, and humidity. In winter, they should be fed a high-calorie diet in order to keep their body temperature slightly above normal. Although they tan, they must be kept out of direct sunlight, which can lead to sunburn.
Unlike other feline breeds, Sphynxes sweat through the skin and should thus be cleaned regularly with a washcloth. Bathing is not advised. The ears must also be cleaned periodically, as they produce a great deal of wax.
Female Sphynxes have no more than two heats per year. The breed has a high rate of neonatal mortality. Sphynx kittens are born with very wrinkled skin and hair along the spine that disappears with age.

(▼)F.I.Fe   (■) L.O.O.F.   (★) C.F.A.   (◆) T.I.C.A.

Turkish Van

Country of Origin:
Turkey
Other Name:
Turkish Swimming Cat

All white with markings on the head and a lovely colored tail

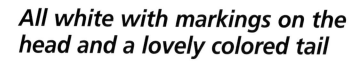

The Turkish Van is a more massive variety of Turkish Angora. It is named for the Lake Van region near Mount Ararat in eastern Turkey. This very old breed was reported as early as the 18th century, but it was not until 1955 that a British breeder named Laura Lushington imported Turkish Vans and truly began breeding them in Europe. The G.C.C.F. and the F.I.Fe. recognized the breed in 1969.

By 1982, the Turkish Van arrived in the United States, where the C.F.A. and T.I.C.A. approved it.

Nevertheless, this breed is quite uncommon in Europe.

Turkish Van

GENERAL
Medium-limbed type, solidly built, fairly massive.
Weight: 3. to 8.5 kg.

COAT
Semilong to long, soft, silky hair without woolly undercoat. Ruff and britches well-furnished in winter. Pure white coat. Reddish-brown (auburn) or cream symmetrical markings at the base of the ears separated by a white blaze. Another colored patch running from the croup to the tip of the tail. The arrangement of these markings is called a "van" pattern. Main recognized colors: red and white, cream and white.

NOTES
Allowable outcross breeds: none.

FAULTS
More than three colored patches on the body. No blaze on the face. Markings unevenly distributed. Tail color starting too far up the back. Disqualify: bicolor and solid patterns. Absence of coloring on the ears and tail.

HEAD
Medium to large in size, at least as long as it is wide. Rounded contours. No angles or straight lines. High cheekbones. Full, rounded muzzle. Nose with slight stop, then delicately hooked (◆). Considerable whisker pinch. Slightly rounded chin.

EARS
Large, broad at the base, set high on the head, with slightly rounded tips.

EYES
Large, shaped like a walnut or peach pit, set slightly at a slant. Eyelids outlined in pink. Color: blue, amber, or heterochromatic. Green is allowed, but amber is preferred.

NECK
Short and strong.

BODY
Long, large, strong. Rounded rib cage. Fairly broad hips. Large-boned, well-developed muscles.

LEGS AND PAWS
Moderately long. Hind legs longer than forelegs. Medium-boned, well-muscled. Round paws. Dense tufts of hair between the toes.

TAIL
Moderately long, thick, well-furnished, fluffy, or plumed. Hair must be at least 5 cm long. The color is even along the entire tail.

<table>
<tr><td></td><td>

CHARACTERISTICS
This particularly hardy, sturdy, very lively cat loves to swim. Although the breed was once reputed to be aggressive, selective breeding has made Turkish Vans friendly, especially toward other cats. Independent, playful, and with a strong character, they are very affectionate and often possessive toward their owner. They are excellent companions and have a moderately loud voice.
</td></tr>
</table>

Turkish Vans can adapt to apartment life, although a large yard with water is better. They grow slowly and take three to five years to reach their full beauty. They require only weekly brushing, except during considerable pre-summer shedding.

(▼)F.I.Fe   (■) L.O.O.F.   (★) C.F.A.   (◆) T.I.C.A.

York Chocolate

A brown-coated city dweller

This new breed created in the United States is named after New York City and its brown coloring. The first York Chocolate kittens were born to housecat parents in the 1980s on Janet Chiefari's farm in New York state. The father was a longhaired black cat, and the mother, also longhaired, was black and white. The old-type Siamese ancestrors of both parents contributed the chocolate gene.

York Chocolate

GENERAL
Old-type Siamese appearance.
Male weighs 7 to 8 kg.
Semilonghaired.

HEAD
Nearly round. Rounded skull. Slightly domed forehead. Moderately long muzzle. Nose without break. Chin in line with tip of nose (■).

EARS
Fairly large, well-spaced. Slightly rounded tips.

EYES
Fairly large, well-spaced, slightly oval, lemon-shaped. Color: gold to green (■).

NECK
Long, thin.

BODY
Long, midway between Oriental and foreign types. Should not be heavy. Fine-boned with slender muscles (■).

LEGS AND PAWS
Long and fine-boned with firm muscles. Small, rounded paws. Long hairs between the toes.

TAIL
Long, thin, straight, tapering to a slender tip. Well-furnished.

COAT
Semilong, fine, soft, silky hair. Very fluffy tail. May have a ruff. Color: solid chocolate, solid lilac, and these same colors in a bicolor version (■). Kittens are much lighter than adults. Tabby markings and tipping are acceptable up to 18 months.

NOTES
Allowable outcross breeds: none.

FAULTS
Head too Oriental in type. Weak chin. Oriental-type eyes. Heavy body. Disqualify: white spots or lockets (■).

CHARACTERISTICS
These lively, energetic cats are good hunters. Playful and affectionate, they are good companions.

(▼) F.I.Fe   (■) L.O.O.F.   (★) C.F.A.   (◆) T.I.C.A.

Pixie Bob

Country of Origin: United States

I n 1985, Carol Ann Brewer, a breeder in Washington state, had a female cat named Pixie who was polydactyl (with more toes than normal). After mating, possibly with a small bobcat, Pixie produced a litter in which some kittens resembled the father (spotted coat, broad ears, etc.). They were called Pixie Bobs. The new breed was recognized by T.I.C.A., which published a standard in 1998. The same year, France also approved the breed.

Pixie Bob

GENERAL
Medium to large in size, slender.
Weight: 4 to 10 kg.
Wild appearance.

HEAD
Broad with prominent forehead. Long, broad muzzle. Very strong chin.

EARS
Broad at the base, rounded at the tips, well-spaced. Lynx tips desirable.

EYES
Slightly oval, moderately deep-set. Color corresponding to that of the coat.

BODY
Long, strong. Prominent shoulders and hips.

LEGS AND PAWS
Long. Muscular. Strong boned. Large paws with fleshy toes. Polydactylism accepted (6-7 toes on the forepaws; 5-6 on the hind paws).

TAIL
Short, thick, flexible.

COAT
Short or long hair. Silky, wooly, resilient, waterproof. Spotted tabby (dark spots on a light background). Well-marked ticking, gray undercoat (◆).

(▼)F.I.Fe   (■) L.O.O.F.   (★) C.F.A.   (◆) T.I.C.A.

CATS AND THEIR
OWNERS

THE SOCIAL ROLE
OF CATS
BEHAVIOR
REARING
DAILY LIFE

Social Function of Cats

A little like "indoor crickets" – a name given to cats because their purring is sometimes as loud as than crickets and cicada put together – cats have come to be recognized as pets in their own right. Moreover, cats are taking over as "man's best friend" in many European countries, France, England, Germany and the United States.

More autonomous and requiring less space, cats have many traits that attract people in this day and age. People who are rushed and stressed find tenderness and understanding in the touch of a cat, with just a hint of the mischievousness and unpredictability that gives cats their special charm.

A Family Affair

Contrary to the typical clichés that portray cats as the companions of choice of writers, night owls and single women, most cat owners are families with two children, a house and a yard. In France, the rate of cat ownership is

A cat and its family

66% among people who live in houses (62% with a yard) and only 25% among apartment dwellers. Sixty-six percent of cats live in cities with a population of fewer than 100,000 people. In this country, there are 8.4 million cats and 1 out of every 4 households has at least one cat. Cats are essentially taken in out of a love for animals. In rare cases, cats are acquired in order to chase mice, but much more often, they are acquired as company for the children. More than 85% of farmers own a cat, followed by merchants, craftsmen and business owners. Only 36% of executives, professional people and unemployed persons share this happiness. Whereas dog owners tend to limit themselves to the canine species, cat owners often own several different species, mixing birds or dogs with cats in their singular love for animals. Although cats have all too often been the poor cousins of veterinary medicine, more attention is being paid to their health in this end of the century, although they still do not receive a lot of medical treatment. In Europe as in the

United States, veterinarians are now specializing in feline medicine and opening up feline clinics. Entire scientific journals are now devoted to this species.

Cats are becoming more strongly attached to people, something thought to be impossible a few centuries ago. Consequently, they are taking on a status similar to dogs: man's faithful friend and first among pets.

In that respect, however, the question remains as to whether cats will ever be truly domesticated. Domestication, in fact, involves controlling reproduction. Herein lies one more paradox with cats. It remains difficult to control the reproduction of thoroughbred cats, who never give birth when the breeders want them to, and yet free-roaming alley and neighborhood cats give birth to litters without a second thought!

Thus the domestication of cats is a work in progress in which we as owners all have the privilege of participating every day.

Cats and Children

Due to preconceived notions and biases, babies and consequently adults, are deprived of the joy of living with a cat. When cats try to jump into the baby's cradle to sleep, the erroneous assumption is made that they have bad intentions and are trying to suffocate the baby.

Two reasons explain why cats are attracted to babies. First, with the baby spitting up curdled milk, the cat cannot help but be attracted to this newfound source of delicacy. This is one reason why cats seek out the cradle, either to lick it or to sleep there. Second, like cats, babies sleep a lot and always in a particularly warm and cozy cradle. In other words, all these temptations bundled into one single being will only serve to attract the cat.

It is wise to keep the cat out of the baby's room during the first few months of life. Care should be taken though to ensure that the cat does not associate the presence of a baby with the absence of attention for him.

During the early development stages, however, both the cat and the baby should be allowed to

A child and her cat

freely interact with each other as they wish. Some mornings, for example, you may see the cat waiting in front of the bedroom door for the baby to wake up. Then he might hop up on the table and offer his flank for a few caresses while the baby eats his breakfast. These types of interaction, which are clearly initiated by the cat, may begin as early as five months. When motor function development begins so do the chasing/running games and the cat may sometimes experience a few difficult moments when the child discovers that his tail moves!

Between the ages of 18 and 24 months young children exhibit the classic aggressive behaviors seen in normal development. During this period, the cat owner must be vigilant and always be nearby when the cat and child interact. Otherwise an unfortunate scratch is always possible. The child must also be taught at this stage to respect the cat, although the cat has his own ways of commanding respect!

For instance, Florence, who at six months was completely fascinated with the dog that would come lick her feet and lie down next to her, clearly began to exhibit inviting behavior and to call out to the cat at the age of eight months. She expressed her pleasure upon seeing the cat with high-pitched shrills and by holding our her hands and smiling in the cat's direction. However, since she did not live with

A teenager and her cat

the cat and only saw it every two weeks, she was not able to "tame" and to handle the cat in the way she wanted until she was two years old.

More so than any other animal, cats can help children make contact with their environment through kinesthetic stimulation and help them to safely explore the immediate environment. Seeing a cat strolling by illicits an immediate and spontaneous response from the child, who cries out to show his joy and excitement, sometimes even forgetting the toothache that kept him awake. These shrieks sometimes cause the cat to run away. This is because both the temperament of the cat and how early or late socialization occurs (which ideally should occur before the age of five weeks), will largely determine the quality and the very nature of the interaction between the child and the cat.

The diversity of feline temperaments also explains why children will not necessarily have the most interactions with the family cat. It may be the grandmother's cat, the older sister's cat or the neighbor's cat that captivates the child and responds to his invitation to interact.

No matter what their age is, children learn to adapt their behavior to the desires of the cat. In short, they learn patience. The cat is a partner who helps them enter the adult world with the help of games.

Quite simply, the cat teaches life skills: patience, respect for others and the ability to control one's gestures and vocal and body expressions.

When Cats Go to School

Some teachers have decided to hire an unusual teaching assistant – a cat. It may be their own cat that lives at the school or a cat they found whose temperament is especially well adapted to their lifestyle.

For example, Sylvie Thevenon tells of her first semester as a young teacher in a Paris neighborhood where discipline was something that was difficult to teach her students.

"The animal arrived unexpectedly a month and a half after school started when one of the children brought in an abandoned cat who had recently been wandering around the newly built school."

From that moment on, the dynamics of the class changed completely. Clearly, nothing could be done that day unless the kitten was included.

All the children began asking questions, wondering if they could keep the cat. They also gave their opinions about the best way to care for it and hold it and, with a very pronounced sense of justice or injustice, about where it should sleep. They thoroughly discussed the "cuddling" time everyone would be allotted.

For once, all the children in the class were expressing themselves and the normal rules of speaking were totally different. They made no references to either the leaders or the teacher! In this respect, the presence of the animal completely changed the behavior of the children. It gave rise to new modes of speaking and listening and gave each student a place, value and a role to play. It brought the class together as a coherent group that was complementary and united by the project. The animal became a true agent of cohesion and it stimulated and motivated that class.

The presence of the animal had numerous consequences throughout the year. Among the most striking was that the children who had trouble concentrating on a task for a long time and who had difficulty situating themselves in time and space discovered that they were able to have projects and stick to them. They improved their concentration skills and became more active and determined. They were also better able to honor their commitments and to accept taking on responsibility. It was almost as if the children "forgot themselves" in the presence of the animal.

The children discussed how to show respect for the animal and how not to bother it. They shared their experiences with their class and also with children in other grades. Stories circulated around the school and works were displayed (little books, poems, drawings, etc.).

For all these reasons, and above all because of the hilarious daily routine that resulted, the presence of the animal became indispensable since it had given the children the opportunity to let others see their true selves without fear of rejection.

The Therapeutic Role of Cats in Hospital Environments

Cats know where hospitals are and many colonies of cats live around hospitals and clinics where the medical staff and often the patients feed and pet them.

Rather than forbidding this practice in the name of hygiene and cleanliness, many doctors and psychiatrists have used their patients' interest in cats to help speed up their recovery or even provide help when traditional medicine fails.

Child psychiatrist Boris Levinson, whose dog Jingles happened by chance to participate in a consultation one day, described the first experiments using animals to facilitate therapy. Normally Levinson did not allow his dog to be in his office. That day, however, he was meeting with parents who were bringing in their autistic son for a last-ditch consultation before most likely having to commit him. Levinson had agreed to see them outside of his usual office hours and his dog stayed in the office. The child said nothing throughout the entire consultation until the very end when the doctor was discussing a second appointment with the parents. The child who had been silent for so long asked if the dog would be there the next time.

From then on, Boris Levinson deliberately used his dog. When he first published his results, he exposed himself to ridicule by his colleagues, who could not resist asking him if he paid his dog.

However, the trend to use pets as therapeutic aids soon began in the United States and eventually took hold in Europe. Dogs were the first animals to be used, but cats are now used regularly for elderly persons and in psychiatric environments.

Obviously, medical personnel who rely on animal-facilitated therapy must use animals with which they have a good rapport. If medical personnel are not familiar with cats or are afraid of them, it is better to choose another species or to refrain from using animals at all. At the Paul-Giraud hospital in Villejuif, France, cats have become invaluable medical assistants under the attentive and affectionate supervision of the medical staff.

"I prefer cats to dogs. We adopt dogs, but cats adopt us. You might say they trust us. They understand us," stated a 58-year old patient who had been receiving care in a specialized unit for over 22 years. Thanks to the presence of cats living around the hospital and to the attentive care of a devoted staff, he was able to get back on track and return to reality. The medical staff plays a very important role because although cats help the patients open themselves up to the world and develop positive behaviors, at the other extreme, it is also possible for patients to become too involved in a relationship that is too exclusive. Cats can be wonderful catalysts for relationships and emotions, but the medical staff must guide

Stray cat

these relationships in order to provide healing, or at least improvement for the patient.

Without getting into the psychiatric aspects, numerous studies have shown that simply petting a cat, talking to it or reading in its presence, without any other special interaction, is enough to lower blood pressure.

Other studies have demonstrated that cardiac patients (those who have suffered from a heart attack or other coronary problems) may live longer in the presence of cats.

Cats can help humanize hospital environments and establish relationships between patients and hospital staff.

All too often, hospital staff members fear that the presence of cats will increase their already heavy workload. However, once cats are brought in, they systematically realize that their presence facilitates their relationships with patients, lessens patient aggressiveness and makes everything easier.

Shared Cats, Garden Nomads

In cities everywhere, wherever cats live in colonies, a network of solidarity, sharing and dialogue is established, which ethnologists are now beginning to study seriously. Women who are sometimes referred to as "cat grannies" help feed these nomadic cats and contribute to maintaining the charm in these places even though they sometimes drive public officials, who want to keep cemeteries clean and well-groomed and free from roaming cats, to

despair. After all, what would the Capitol, the Forum of Rome or the Père-Lachaise cemetery be without cats? They would undoubtedly be places without a soul.

This situation is well accounted for in the new pet protection law published at the beginning of 1999, which henceforth establishes true protection laws for these free-roaming cats. Sterilized, identified, and sometimes vaccinated whenever possible, these cats can now stroll along with confidence under our delighted gaze. Just like with those who feed the pigeons, there are people who take great delight in caring for cats they cannot take into their homes. The cats repay them well as they are generous with their affection.

Cats and the Elderly

Cats make excellent pets for elderly persons for all the reasons stated above, but also because they are so autonomous. Nevertheless, it is important to choose a good-natured cat that is not to lively and that is well socialized if children will be visiting regularly.

Longhaired cats should be avoided because they require daily brushing and sometimes-daily eye care. But there again, it all depends on the nature of the elderly person or couple.

Of course there is still the painful problem that sometimes prevents an elderly person from enjoying the company of a cat. And that is the question of, "But what about after I am gone, Dr.?"

This desire to ensure that the cat continues to live a comfortable life even after the person

---

BUSINESS CATS – THE PROFESSION OF THE FUTURE

Trends from the United States have more chance of taking root here if they fulfill genuine expectations. For a long time now, many merchants and even post offices have let their cats wander around in their shop or office. Today, media and advertising agencies do not think twice about allowing their employees to bring their dogs to work. Since cats do not especially like being transported, when businesses have a cat, the cat generally lives there and becomes the office mascot. Cats are used to veterinary offices, but they can also work for big companies, where they clearly change the atmosphere and create an environment of cohesion around them.

dies is entirely understandable. The concern is especially valid in cases where the elderly person lives alone or is a widow. A friendly "adoption" arrangement is the best solution to keep from depriving an elderly person of this daily dose of happiness. After all, how many cleaning women, household assistants, friends or relatives would contribute to giving the elderly person a sense of security by promising to look after the cat if it has the sad surprise of seeing its master gone on before him…

Often, elderly persons will not be able to enjoy the company of one or more cats with their mind at ease unless they have this guarantee. However, the children or grandchildren of these persons should not feel guilty if they cannot take on such a commitment. There are enough cat lovers out there to testify to human solidarity and their ability to share.

Bear in mind, nevertheless, that for both young and old alike, the death of a cat is a particularly sensitive time. It may even lead to depression or illness in cases of people who are fragile or sick (people suffering from multiple sclerosis, for example). Those in the entourage of the grieving person should be sure to provide plenty of support for him or her. The grieving process is especially difficult for elderly persons who have already lost a spouse and for whom the cat was the only living testimony to their life together. The same holds true for adolescents whose parents are divorced and who just lost the cat that sometimes was the only memory of their parents' marriage and their childhood. Pay close attention to loved ones in these situations and support them in difficult times. "The pain of a cat, is pain all the same."

Cat Rearing and Behavior

In spite of their reputation for being independent and autonomous, cats can be trained at a young age and they exhibit a clear aptitude for learning. Take as but one example the case of a kitten that was reared with young puppies and that learned by imitation to lift its leg to urinate! Nevertheless, kittens can only be taught natural behavior sequences, which can be either positively or negatively reinforced and thereby shape their behavior. The extremely rare artists who work with cats in circus environments have to rely on pure art. They take note of their cat's interesting behaviors, reinforce these behaviors and then display them on scene in order to enhance their value. Motivation is almost more important with cats than with dogs. Furthermore, motivation in this case means the same as motivation with humans. In other words, the cat has to want to do something in order to do it. Pavlov's beloved method of using food as bait for motivation, which was so effective with dogs, is not so effective with cats. A cat's attachment to his master and his love of games are sources of motivation that are a thousand times more effective. The fact that neurophysiologists even refer to the notion of motivation shows the degree of intelligence they attribute to cats.

Rearing a Kitten

Advanced knowledge about feline behavior now indicates that psychomotor development begins with gestation, thus before birth, just as with humans. The behavior of the mother will influence the behavior of her future kittens and their abilities to learn.

A team of British researchers also proved that sociability towards humans may be genetically determined and may be a character trait that kittens inherit from their fathers. For now, this is the only influence the father is known to have on his offspring, since he does not care for the kittens after they are born.

The bulk of learning occurs nevertheless during the period from birth to six months.

Training and learning are also possible as adults, depending on the temperament of the cat and the teaching skills of the owner.

With kittens, behavior takes shape around three main hubs within the litter:
- learning, which plays an important role;
- the role of the mother, which is more and more seen as being important at the very beginning of development;
- socialization, which will determine to a large extent how a kitten behaves as an adult.

In fact, we even talk about intra-specific socialization, which means establishing all the communication behaviors specific to the feline species. These behaviors are established very early on, especially as compared to dogs, and they are essential to the proper develop-

Kittens in a Group

ment of the kitten and his emotional stability. They begin to be established around the second week after birth and continue until the seventh week, sometimes a little longer.

During this period, it is important to provide kittens with what ethnologists call "an enriched environment." In other words, they need specific sources of stimuli that will arouse their senses and spark their intelligence.

Contact and games with other kittens are essential to development before the age of eight weeks. Inter-specific socialization, the process of learning social behaviors directed toward other friendly species (humans, dogs, rabbits, etc.), also occurs during this period and ends around the third month. The nature and strength of the bond that develops between the cat and his owner will depend on the quality of this inter-specific socialization. It is possible to influence the sociability of a cat by having various people handle the kitten during the first few weeks of life. This will make for a good-natured cat. The cat will learn to adapt to everyone, but overall, will not be extremely attached to one person in particular. Conversely, the kitten can be handled by only one or two people maximum, which will consequently make for a cat with only one master, who will be extremely attached to his future owner.

Cats must also be taught about other species they will later have to live with at a young age, as it will be infinitely more difficult to familiarize them later on. This is especially true for toddlers who, in the eyes of the cat, are an entirely separate breed from the human race! It is sometimes difficult for cats to accept young children, who are unpredictable, able to emit very shrill sounds, and to take advantage of the moment when adults are not paying attention to pull on the whiskers, tail or ears of a passing cat. It is important to familiarize cats with young children, especially in cases of grandparents who only have the children over from time to time.

Grooming, feeding (after weaning) and defecating and urinating behaviors are certainly all inborn to some degree, but the mother also teaches them to kittens soon after birth. Around the 15th day, kittens are capable of licking their front sides. Starting at three weeks, kittens can answer the call of nature in a litter box on their own. As of the fourth

Example of a Maine Coon in an enriched environment.

week, kittens are able to eat the same food as their mother, imitating her behavior and acquiring her food preferences in so doing. Kittens also learn to drink fresh water at this age. As the taste of water is different from the taste of milk, it is important to train them quickly.

In order to prevent the cat from becoming a finicky eater, it is important to give young kittens foods with different textures and tastes (dry food, croquettes and pâtés with different flavors).

At Home with the Owner

When a young kitten is adopted, its training is limited. The kitten is normally already house broken and generally, the owner needs simply show the kitten the litter box once and the kitten will remember where it is and come back to it systematically.

The kitten also learns, for no apparent reason, where the refrigerator and everything else that gives him access food is located!

It is more difficult to train a cat not to bother the table and your dishes and food. In fact, it is normal behavior for cats to jump up on the table or the kitchen work space. If you wish to eliminate this behavior, a sharp "no" will suffice. You may accompany that with a sharp sound (snapping your fingers or clapping your hands).

If, however, the cat is normally allowed to jump up on the table and to walk on the table, it is extremely difficult to keep it off a table set for guests. All you can do in this case is shut the dining room door!

Giving the cat unrestricted access to all rooms in the house is generally the simplest way to operate. Nevertheless, it is easy to restrict access to the baby's room, although the rules must be established at the right time, in other words, one month before the baby is born.

Social Behavior

As paradoxical as it may seem, cats are social animals. Even though they sometimes prefer to avoid contact (especially with some of their congeners), cats do show a true talent for communication with humans in optimal living conditions.

Nature has given cats particularly subtle and varied means of communication, which enable them to detect the presence and emotional state of other cats or animals. They can therefore make an informed decision about whether to approach the other animal or not.

When an encounter with a congener is unavoidable and not desired, all means of communication are deployed in a dissuasive strategy where bluffing is the name of the game.

Since cats are basically visual animals, they are especially sensitive to contrasts in light (they can distinguish differences of 10 – 12%) and to movement. They are able to detect a mouse moving at the ridiculous rate of 144 m/hr.

"ENRICHED ENVIRONMENT"

Buried in this conventional term is simply the idea of raising kittens in a diverse environment with respect to physical space, senses and relationships. All studies have shown the benefits for kittens who are exposed, even if only for a few minutes a day, to diverse objects (little balls, brown paper bags, cardboard boxes, etc.) and to pieces of wood on which they can climb. There should be objects big enough for them to hide in (cardboard boxes are a veritable gold mine!) as well as various sounds (television, children playing and crying, music, etc.). Kittens raised in these conditions showed preliminary signs of play well before the age of five weeks (the normal age for these activities). Their development was clearly accelerated and greatly improved.

The objective of having an enriched environment is to promote harmonious behavioral development in kittens and to enable them to adapt in any circumstance. Kittens raised in this manner have well-developed exploratory behaviors.

Color is not a decisive factor for cats. They can only detect blue and green with certainty. Contrary to common thought, cats are not able to see in complete darkness. However, they require six times less light than humans do to distinguish an object with the same degree of clarity. This means that they distinguish beings and depth better than humans do at night.

Moreover, their whiskers provide an excellent additional source of information because they provide keen detection of objects thanks to gradients in heat and turbulence, which direct their nose and taste buds to the most favorable angle.

The final olfactory advantage cats have is their vomer-nasal passage, which links the buccal cavity and the nasal cavity. At the top of this passage is the Jacobson's organ, which is lined with olfactive cells that are directly linked by nerve pathways to olfactory bulb. Because of this anatomical particularity, cats are considered to be macrosmic (animals that can detect a single odorant molecule whereas humans require several hundred). Cats therefore have a keen sense of smell and thus, emotions.

Cats are generally thought to have a musical ear. They can detect differences of one tenth in high frequency tones and difference of one fourth in average frequency tones. It is also clear that in familiar settings, cats respond to their name and can distinguish their name from other names in the family. Most likely they are also responding to the voice tone and intonation of their owner because if it happens to be the veterinarian saying their name at his office, cats generally remain stone faced, once again proving their attachment to their owner. Although cats can subtly analyze the behavior of others, they also allow their emotions to show, either directly or by leaving traces of their path. This deferred, or distance communication essentially involves leaving deposits of odors and visual marks.

Odor deposits, which include urine and feces deposits and sudoriferous gland secretions, are

WHAT IS THE TEMPERAMENT OF THE CAT?

This question was incongruous just several decades ago but now, thanks to studies on colonies of free-roaming cats, we know that cats have different temperaments:
-the suspicious cat: always on the alert, on the defensive, does not explore a lot of unknown territory, does not interact with unknown congeners, runs from human strangers;
- the sociable cat: always likes contact (mutual licking, social games), seeks out and initiates contact;
- the intermediary cat: neither sociable, nor suspicious, responds to solicitations even from strangers but does not initiate contact, not an active communicator but has an even-keel temperament.

A child playing with her cat.

THE BREEDER – A SECOND MOM

As the inescapable middleman between the kitten and his future owner, the breeder and his/her family play a big role in determining the behavior of a kitten. The breeder is the "human reference" for the kitten.

This is one reason why whenever cats are destined for families with young children, it is important between the second and seventh week for the kitten to have contact either with the young children he will be living with (even if only once a week) or with other children close to the breeder. This may seem tedious or complicated, but it is nonetheless the best way to end up with a kitten that is perfectly adapted to his future life. The same holds true for cats that will have to live with dogs in their adult life. It is important that the breeder himself have dogs or that he be able to put his litters in contact with good-natured dogs.

Systematic handling can deepen the future bond between kitten and human. The kitten is handled everyday during the socialization period (picked up, pet and talked to for 5 – 40 minutes per day). If the breeder does the handling himself, the kitten will bond more easily with an owner who is single. If the kitten will go to live with a family, two or three different people, preferably of each sex, should do the handling. These people should also have as good a relationship with kittens and the mother cat as the breeder. If the mother cat is fearful, it is preferable to do the handling when she is not present.

Cats use five main postures to communicate:
1. *Friendly*
2. *Confrontational*
3. *Defensive*
4. *Aggressive*
5. *Threatening*

often referred to as "marking." It should be noted, however, that the very notion of marking presupposes that the odor deposit instills fear and causes the one who just smelled it to flee. This is the case with most Felidae, but with cats on the contrary, the odor deposit, especially if it is a urine deposit, incites the passerby to cover over this deposit with another deposit and to continue on his way without fear. Consequently, the term odor deposits is more accurate as it does not make assumptions about the function of this behavior.

Recently, some of these substances were isolated and synthesized in the form of a spray. The sprays were reported to have a calming effect, but at any rate they cannot solve everything. In cases of behavioral problems, it is always important to seek the advice of your veterinarian.

Cats also leave their mark by scratching trees, furniture and sometimes the edge of the sofa. Several theories have been proposed. Some see this scratching as simply an original form of stretching. The cat stretches, especially upon

awakening, and scratches anything that happens to get in the way of his paws. Others believe that when a cat scratches an object, it leaves secretions from the small glands located between the plantar pads. These glands are activated by fear, especially when the cat is at the veterinarian's office, and cat therefore leave their mark as well as visual traces in the form of slashes in softer material (leather sofas are often left in a sorry state!).

The latter theory explains why commercial scratching posts do not work well. They do not convey a story. It is of course through direct communication that cats show their true talent as comedians and bluffers and sometimes their sense of tragedy.

When cats encounter other cats, they use postures and vocal sounds and they transmit subtle messages to the other cat through movement of their whiskers and ears.

There are five main postures, depending on the emotions of the cat and the messages he wishes to communicate.

The arched "cat back" is the best known posture and the term is even used in everyday language. In this posture, the cat makes itself appear as frightening as possible. Its fur stands on end to make it look larger, his tail is puffed out like a bottlebrush and its pupils are extremely dilated.

Conversely, during a friendly encounter its fur lies flat and its tail is bent in characteristic fashion.

When a cat is in a threatening position: crouched down, growling, and with its claws extended, it is important not to interpret this posture as being a posture of submission as with dogs. In this position, the cat is ready to do anything to get out of the bad situation in which he finds himself and it will bite if the other party persists.

Fights between cats are always spectacular to hear. In fact, there is often a lot of noise for nothing, which is just fine. Except for fights between male cats during mating season, when biting is serious, cat fights are more often than not merely long periods of waiting and preparing for battle backed up by growling. When the attack is launched, it is brief and lively,

larger than normal hair and is embedded in a sanguineous sinus, which creates hydraulic suspension. Their sensitivity to the slightest movement of air is therefore amplified.

Arranged in groups of four or five in four rows around the nose, the whiskers change position according to the activities and emotions of the cat. During waking activities (chasing, lying in wait or friendly encounters), the whiskers are positioned in a arch of a circle. They are quickly pulled down during an attack. There are also vibrissa above the carp under the anterior side of the forelegs, just above the eyes and a few tufts on the jowls.

Well Adapted Communication Strategies

At least three different personalities live inside the head of the cat:

- the hunter: very discrete, wants to see without being seen, moves silently;
- the show-off: struts around during mating season, removes intruders from its path by arching its back and makes more noise than the others in order to protect its secret garden. A devilish bluffer, it does nonetheless step aside sometimes, since the rule among cats is to give the right of way to the first one to arrive;
- the charmer: has taken up residence with humans for good, its needs are provided for (food), it is sheltered from the worries of living with others, it has all the time in the world to develop specific behaviors that would normally not be expressed except in these particular living conditions. Purring, kneading behavior, social licking behavior (licking the eyebrows

punctuated by impressive vocal sounds, and then it is over as soon as it began.

These behaviors are frequently seen in games between two adult cats living together. Only experience will tell if it is really just a game or whether you need to take one of your cats to the veterinarian to be treated for aggression. When cats chase something or lick themselves, their ear pinna may be flipped back in order to obtain information, but they are always perfectly straight.

Finally, it is not unusual to see that the ears are not symmetrical in their movements. This is because cats do not have "eyes in back of their heads" and they skillfully use the stereophonic gifts nature has given them and also because they are generally apt to change moods and the movement of their ears indicates the slightest variation.

Whiskers are a form of vibrissa, the hair that is distinctly characteristic of mammals (except humans). The whisker base is five to six times

Neutral cat

Angry cat

Aggressive cat

Happy cat

EARS AND WHISKERS – VALUABLE INDICATORS

Ear movements are sometimes the only indication of a cat's emotions. Equipped with a well-controlled musculature, the ears position themselves according to the whims of the cat's moods, which can vary from one minute to the next. Straight up, pointing slightly forward, moving or working independently (it is not unusual to see that only one ear turns toward the source of a noise), they indicate a cat that feels confident, as he takes in information about the surrounding environment. When the pinna are facing forward or when the ears are pointing toward the source of a sound, they indicate that the cat is on the alert. In situations when cats are on the defensive, the ears lie flat laterally and are perfectly symmetrical, giving their forehead the characteristic smooth, bulged out appearance, and betraying intense anxiety. When the pinna are pulled back, it is already too late – aggression has already started (see pictures as shown opposite).

of his owner when he comes home at night) and vocal sounds so rich and expressive that they are taken at their word, are all signs of domestication and its consequences.

Cats organize their lives around different areas. They have areas for resting, eating, eliminating waste, and playing. There is also a temporary area for reproduction. If the cat is free roaming, there is a hunting area, which can be quite a large area (several hectares).

Respecting this organization can avoid a lot of problems. Not respecting these areas on the other hand, can be the source of many behavioral problems.

In an apartment, it is important for the elimination area to be as far as possible from the eating area. The resting area will vary depending on the amount of sunshine and the mood of the cat. The proximity of the owner or one of his family members also plays a role. Cats always look for sources of heat (radiators, comforters) and it is not unusual to see a cat sleeping next to the fireplace or on a piping hot radiator. Since cats are less sensitive to heat than humans, they take enjoy it as much as possible.

The play area is the biggest area in their field of investigation because it is during their crazy chases (where they alone know what they are actually chasing) that they cover the most ground. Cats are particularly fond of high up places (such as the table or the top of the wardrobe) and the climbing they require. Cats are filled with joy when they can be at the same level as their owner's, face allowing them to have their own style "cat-to-cat" interaction by rubbing against their owner's cheek or forehead just like they would with another cat.

Eating Behaviors

Gourmet by nature, cats owe many of their habits to their Egyptian ancestors and domestication.

Felis lybica and Felis ornata are the two most likely ancestors of the cat. Originally from the desert, they both had few opportunities to drink and had to be satisfied with the meager prey they often hunted, which was essentially mice.

Cats have maintained this sobriety in terms of water (even though in actual fact they drink more than we think) and have stayed in the habit of eating many small meals in a twenty-four hour period. Thus, cats eat ad libitum and may eat as many as 15 – 16 meals, consuming an average of eight grams per meal. The time spent eating is always very short – 15 minutes total per day. But the frequency with which they come to their feeding dish, which is generally when the owner is nearby, leads one to believe that all they do is eat!

POISONS

Among the most frequent causes of poisoning are:

- Organophosphorous and carbamate insecticides: salivating, vomiting, diarrhea and convulsions;
- Organochlorine insecticides: hyperactivity, vomiting and convulsions;
- Antifreeze (ethylene glycol): vomiting, cardiac problems, convulsions, coma and death;
- Anticoagulants (dicoumarol, antivitamin K): lethal internal hemorrhaging;
- Paracetamol (toxic starting at 50 – 60 mg/kg): loss of appetite, vomiting and jaundice;
- Aspirin (toxic starting at 25 mg/kg): vomiting, depression, coma and death;
- "Toxic" plants which, when ingested, can cause:
    - Digestive problems: ficus, mistletoe, holly, rhododendron, azalea, etc.;
    - Kidney problems: philodendron, ficus;
    - Cardiovascular problems: cylclamen, mistletoe;
    - Nervous system problems: mistletoe, Japanese mimosa, and philodendron.

Some cats prefer to eat at night, others spread their meals out over regular intervals and still others prefer to eat during the official mealtimes of the family.

As the ultimate nibblers, cats come back to their dish often to savor a small mouthful. Note that their digestive system is perfectly adapted to this eating pattern and that cats generally do not tolerate being fed once a day very well, unlike dogs.

The ideal system, both in terms of cats' pleasure and their health, seems to be to distribute dry food ad libitum along with fresh water, and to give them pâté or croquettes twice a day.

Cats are only moderate water drinkers. They drink nine to ten times a day, drinking about 12.6 ml each time. They are highly sensitive to odors and they hate plastic dishes that retain bad odors. They prefer glass or heavy porcelain dishes by far.

Some unconventional cats like to drink directly from the tap, sometimes using their paw. Others are particularly fond of bath water, but the main source of water should always come from the owner!

As an "informed consumer," cats assumedly control their food intake according to their needs. Statistics show in fact that only 6 – 12% of the feline population is obese as opposed to 20 – 30% among canines. Nevertheless, it is necessary to be reasonable and to limit the overall amount of food a cat consumes in a day, even if the food is distributed in self-service style.

As for the variety of food to give the cat's palate, your cat will let you know! Reputed to be difficult by some of the advertising agencies, some cats do prove to be loyal to a certain brand, texture or even a certain flavor throughout their entire life.

It is clear nonetheless that unlike a dog, a cat would rather starve to death than eat something he does not like. Therefore, you are not giving into the cat's every whim by buying different flavors and varieties. That being said, a kitten's palate can be trained. This is done by first giving the mother and then later the kit-tens food that is varied in texture (pâtés, canned food and dry food) and in flavor when the litter is weaned from the mother. This practice will make for easy-going cats.

Waste Elimination Behavior

House training is one of the behaviors closely associated with cats. It is a behavior that is acquired very early on, from the 22nd to the 39th day. Prior to this time, cats respond to stimulation by their mother, who licks the anal-genital area after each feeding in order to stimulate urination and defecation.

True neurological control over this behavior is not fully operational until three to four weeks. At 30 days, kittens begin to approach the litter box or loose dirt for the first time. The behavioral sequence is triggered soon after and the kittens scratch the litter, eliminate and then cover their feces. Among especially meticulous cats, the latter part of the sequence can sometimes reach the walls of the litter box itself, making the noise they clearly wanted to hear!

Contrary to what happens with dogs, there is no noticeable difference between male and female elimination behavior. Both eliminate by crouching down. If your cat emits a strong spray of urine horizontally, he is not relieving himself, but rather depositing his odor.

Any elimination in an inappropriate place (sink, shower stall, bedroom, etc.) should be checked out for possible behavioral problems.

Grooming Behaviors

Along with sleep, grooming is probably one of the cat's biggest activities, to such an extent that Pasteur is credited with saying, "cats are clean animals because they spend all day grooming themselves."

In addition to the cleaning function in the strict sense of the word, grooming has an important calming effect. When cats lick themselves or when they are licked by another (as with kittens licked by their mother), endorphin production is triggered, the same

WHY DO CATS OFTEN EAT GRASS?

This frequent behavior is not a cause for alarm. In nature, wild carnivores do not eat only meat. Their diet is also partly made up of vegetables in order to maintain a balanced diet and provide them with a source of energy. A cat that eats grass, therefore, is simply replicating an ancestral behavior, even if its diet is otherwise perfectly balanced. Undoubtedly, cats are also sensitive to some of the tastes and odors of grass. Nonetheless, even though grass is said to be a purgative, it is important to have your cat de-wormed regularly in order to eliminate intestinal parasites.

British Blue cats (mother cat and kitten) during grooming.

hormones that are produced to counteract the sensation of pain. An anxious cat, for example, will lick itself more frequently than another cat, even at the risk of mutilating itself and pulling out hair.

Because it can be done to others, the licking behavior has a social function that is clearly illustrated in the mother-kitten relationship. Functional as of the 15th day of life, grooming is done with the particularly rough tongue and also with the paws. The front paw is moistened with the tongue and then serves as a sort of washcloth to reach the ears. The back paws are used to reach the ears and the back, sometimes with a little too much zeal. We can see the classic autopodal reflex – the paws begin to move when the side of a parasite-infected ear, typically mange, is scratched. However, we may also see another, non-pathological reflex when we stroke the cat's lower back – the cat's tongue makes licking movements in time with the stroking!

Reproductive Behaviors

Cats reach puberty at an early age – around six months and sometimes even earlier if they are exposed to a lot of sun. Thus kittens born in the spring are less precocious than kittens born at the beginning of summer. The latter kittens will have their first heat at the beginning of January or February, depending on the weather

Mother cat nursing her kittens

conditions. If cats are not purebreds and if you do not want them to reproduce, it is preferable to have them spayed as soon as possible based on the advice of your veterinarian. Moreover, since some infectious diseases can be transmitted through biting, which occurs frequently when tomcats fight, it is pointless to expose your cat to additional risks if you do not want to carry on his line. In addition, studies on female cats have clearly shown that early sterilization can help prevent breast tumors later on. Some owners believe it is useful for their female cat to have one litter before being spayed, even if it means killing the kittens. This is utterly cruel for the mother cat and there is no scientific basis for it. Of course the maternity experience is extremely gratifying for both the mother and her owner when the pregnancy is desired. But it is not based on any biological or behavioral imperative.

Cats are mature between the ages of 6 and 12 months. Hormonal secretions give the male cat facial aspects that are different from a pre-pubescent cat or a neutered cat. His cheeks develop to the point where they can truly be called jowls and he generally becomes lanky at the same time when female cats are in heat, from spring to the beginning of autumn because both chasing the she-cats and fighting with other males are exhausting. Frequently, these fights result in abscesses, which require a visit to the veterinarian for an appropriate treatment (prescription of antibiotics and in some cases, surgery in order to lance the abscess and allow the puss to drain).

Female cats can first start gestation as of the age of five months. However, as a precaution, it is recommended to wait until she is eight or nine months old. The period of heat, which lasts four to eight days, is followed by a period of rest for eight to ten days. If the cat does not become pregnant, this cycle will continue to repeat itself from spring through autumn.

One biological peculiarity is that ovulation in the female cat is triggered by mating, which means that mating must occur several times in a row in order to have successful fertilization. This practice can lead to kittens from the same litter with different fathers.

A female cat does not allow a male to approach her unless she is receptive. When she is receptive, she first meows languorously and plays the "untouchable tease" by rubbing her nose and lips on the ground and rolling on the ground. She makes a characteristic vocal sound, sometimes repeatedly, with a distressing and uneasy cry.

Mating is always an impressive sight to behold for the novice, but opportunities to witness it are relatively rare, since the frolicking preferably occurs at night.

Generally, the female has calmly watched the fights that the males start over her pretty eyes. After the fights, she does not necessarily choose the most courageous male, as has been shown in recent studies.

In response to her cry, the male makes a characteristic meow in a low, diphthong voice after having copiously sprayed the encounter spot with his urine. The female then adopts a suitable position, lying flat on the ground with her croup lifted. Her tail moves to one side opening up the anal-genital zone. Coitus occurs fleetingly, and the female reacts violently. The male penis is equipped with little spines that help stimulate the vagina but can also be painful. The female may turn toward the male violently and sometimes bites him. A female can be covered more than seven times. The ensuing ovulation does not automatically suppress the heat behavior.

Nothing in life prepares the female cat for the upheaval associated with gestation and yet, in 99% of cases, she adopts a maternal behavior with her young that is always admirable. Gestation lasts from 58 – 71 days. Before giving birth, the cat looks for a warm, cozy place such as the bottom of a wardrobe, a straw basket or a shoebox. She should be left in peace for the big moment. The mother cuts the umbilical cord herself and eats the placenta surrounding each kitten. Since the placenta is so rich, she will not be hungry again for one or two days after giving birth. As soon as they are born, each kitten heads for a breast and will always return to the same one for three to four weeks.

Just because the mother is nursing does not mean that she cannot be in heat again, some-times as soon as 15 days after giving birth. Therefore if you only want to have one litter, plan to have your veterinarian perform surgery as soon as possible. This will not bother the kittens in any way once they reach the age of three weeks.

Since ancient times, cats have had the reputation of being fertile and prolific. Some cats continue to be fertile well past the age of 13 or 14 years. Tri-colored cats have the reputation of being able to give birth to three litters per year. The average is generally around two, with four to six kittens per litter.

Locomotive Behavior

Tightrope walkers without equal, cats are like artists working without a net, whether they are climbing down out of a tree as fast as a high-speed train, or climbing on your knees.

Their natural ease stems from several gifts: joint and muscle flexibility, an unequaled sense of balance and excellent vision that enables them to locate obstacles.

As swift as a horse, cats can adopt a gait in two or four stages and walk at four different paces: walking, ambling, trotting and galloping.

Climbing is child's play for them even on seemingly smooth surfaces. His claws are powerful allies even though cats that have been de-clawed seem to manage quite well.

Cats always know how to get back down the same way they came up, unless they become frightened at the top and the shouts of the owner, who is even more scared, prevents them from using their skills to get back down. Pay attention to the risks involved in attempting to get a cat down from a tree or another delicate situation. Scratching can occur and the cat will hold on tightly to his rescuer, sometimes with a death grip.

Finally, the popular notion that cats always land on their feet is a myth. Granted with anything above the seventh floor, the cat will fall at a constant speed and his injuries will not be any more serious. But unfortunately, they often suffer fractures or pneumothorax at this altitude that can seriously endanger their life.

The falling cat test

A cat purring with pleasure in the arms of its owner.

two heights, some parachutist cats manage to escape unharmed while others end their lives prematurely. Be careful with balconies, especially in cities, where pigeons and other birds can tempt the cat to stick its nose out a little farther than it should.

In contrast to humans, it was thought that animals had only their instincts to go by until the XVIIIth century. At the opposite extreme, the notion of cat intelligence was exaggerated and confused with what was simple learning (complex though it may be) and true intelligence (according to J.-P. Chaurand in *Le Comportement du chat et ses troubles* [Cat Behavior and Problems], ed. du Point Vétérinaire, 1995).

A True Actor

Like a situation comedy with all kinds of humor, cats are never without ideas. They put on a pitiful face if mealtime is missed, loiter about their empty dish, look their owner straight in the eye and meow. Their voice is husky, coming from deep down. It is the cry of a beggar. Then they turn into a tramp, checking out trashcans with their nostrils wide open. It would be surprising if they did not find an old bone, a few scraps of ham or the leftover meat of the youngest child who does not like

At anything under one and a half meters, a cat does not have time to turn around and ends up falling on one body part or another and damaging it. With anything in between these

---

PURRING: THE MYSTERY OF HOW IT IS TRIGGERED PERSISTS

Purring is a murmur specific to Felidae that a cat emits when its mouth is closed, causing a sound and a laryngeal vibration. It expresses an intense emotional state, which could be pleasure or pain. Some cats that are in the terminal phase of cancer or that suffered from a traffic accident purr intensely, expressing their pain and anxiety. For a long time, it was believed that purring came from a specific organ. Actually purring is an aerodynamic phenomena made possible by coordinated movements of the glottis and larynx and the adjacent muscles. Nevertheless, purring is still a voluntary behavior that humans cannot activate intentionally. Petting generally stimulates purring, but not always.

Since kittens purr more frequently than adults, it is now believed that purring is a means for the cat to express dependence on its mother, and more generally, on the person caring for it (owner, veterinarian or veterinarian's aid). With domestic cats, purring can become a means of communication with humans. Up to you to figure out what the cat is trying to tell you!

beef steak. At any rate the cat always has a solution – the closet! With one swipe of the paw, it knocks down the whole pile of little tarts and dry food. One would have to be deaf not to react to this cataclysm.

Another place where the cat reveals its humor: the litter box. Has the litter not been changed?

It walks around its toilet, sniffs it, steps one foot in and immediately takes it out of this foul heap of odors that is a magnet for a diseases of all sorts like a devil on springs. However, there are also scenes where the cat has no humor. If it misses a landing while doing its acrobatic feats, it is ashamed and hides in a corner out of sight and licks itself for a long time, focusing his energy on this substitute grooming, which is an attitude specific to cats when they are ill at ease…

ANIMAL INTELLIGENCE TESTS

- The lowest level on the scale consists of assessing an animal's ability to establish a relationship between two events or between one event and the response that it is supposed to give.
This in itself is learning at varying degrees of complexity.
- The highest level consists of subjecting the cat to a series of problems (finding food, for example), that are all different, but that have one point in common that it can latch onto if it discovers it. The experiment therefore measures how long it takes for the cat to improve its performance and to stop making errors in situations that are different each time. There are many variations on this test and in particular, one called the "inversion" test.
Food is hidden under one of two objects first, then under the other. This test can also be done with three objects, which makes it particularly difficult. The alternation between the two objects is always the same during the various problems to which the cat is successively exposed. If it shows an improvement in his performance during the last series of tests, it is clear that it has grasped the common element in all these problems.
Another series of tests consists of asking the animal to find means of obtaining food. In the case of a chimpanzee, for example, boxes are stacked up so that it may climb on top of them and reach a bunch of bananas.
Motivation is sometimes a problem when it comes to experiments with cats. When they are in their natural environment, we observe very elaborate behaviors. For example, Nounours, the European cat, had been designated by its four housemates to jump from the table onto the refrigerator and with a swipe of the paw, knock the package of dry food on the ground for the enjoyment of the other cats who were then able to calmly eat it. Nounours was also in charge of opening the door, a task at which it excelled.
Despite the inherent limits to their validity, all these tests and trials help establish a system to rank the degree of animal intelligence. Ranked at the top are primates and Rhesus monkeys, with cats falling somewhere in the upper average.

Cats
and Daily Life

Even though Moncrif wrote in 1727 that "by virtue of their meticulous cleanliness, cats could teach us a lesson or two," and although according to Pasteur "cats are the only clean animals" in creation, cats do nonetheless require some care on a daily basis.

Daily Life

As a factor that determines quality of life, a cat's familiar environment should always be looked after. Of course that does not mean you need to wait until you move into Versailles in order to enjoy living with a cat. But, as in many other areas, cats always prefer quality to quantity.

Indoor cat

In an Apartment

Granted, 25m² seems to be a minimal space for an apartment cat. However, even reduced to this limited space, a cat owner can still provide the cat what it needs to savor its favorite joys – high altitude surveillance and daily stretching – by adding a few shelves, maybe a wardrobe that is not too high and a nice scratching post (sometimes an old tree trunk will do the trick better than a patented scratching post).

The cleanliness of the litter box is crucial to prevent behavioral problems associated with house-training, especially in small spaces where odors can spread easily.

Some owners are able to successfully train their cat to answer the call of nature on the balcony (if they have one). However, this practice requires that the cat control its desire to jump up on the edge of the balcony with all the risks involved. Depending on the specific abilities of each cat, the owner can give the cat more or less freedom, but most often he should supervise the cat.

Even the most acrobatic of cats is not entirely protected from a fall caused when he thought he could catch a bird flying or an even more nasty fall when it gets carried away chasing an infrared light… Just like with babies during bath time, caution and supervision are strongly recommended when cats are on the balcony.

In a House

If the house has several floors, it is wise to place a litter box on every level, even if the cat lives alone without any other cats. This will facilitate the life of your cat and prevent annoying accidents.

If there are several cats, it is preferable to set up as many litter boxes as cats (up to a reasonable limit of four boxes). Frequently, all the cats use the same litter box even if some boxes are reserved for urine and others are only for defecation.

Of course, the ideal (for the person cleaning the house, that is) would be for cats to have the brilliant idea to answer the call of nature outside, but this behavior is not always given, as evidenced by the pleasure some cats take in coming back inside to urinate or defecate in their litter box. Summer is obviously the best time to try to inculcate these good manners, especially since in the winter cats are too lazy to go out!

Generally speaking, cats deal well with the daily absence of their owner because their sleep patterns are often timed with our working hours.

Moreover, even though cats are often very attached to their masters, they seem to have more emotional autonomy than their friends the dogs, and the anxiety separation disorders classically seen in dogs is rarely seen in cats. This may be explained by the fact that it is also true that cat owners have fewer departure rituals than dog owners do.

Whether cats live in an apartment or in a house, they need to be protected from a certain number of household accidents.

Green plants are among the temptations that should be extracted from Mr. Cat's teeth, especially if the plant appears to be toxic in nature (see attached list).

You could, on the other hand, arrange harmless plants in such a way that the cat will be attracted to them and will spare your other plants.

This strategy can also be applied to the garden, where sometimes the cat's talents as a gardener are not fully appreciated, especially when it plows up the freshly-sown seedbed or decides to attend to the call of nature in the impatiens freshly planted that morning.

A lot could be gained by planting a small corner of Labiatae (thyme, mint and catnip – but be sure to ask for the real stuff because some seed vendors have the annoying habit of selling wild oats in place of catnip and calling it "catmint."), along with couch grass to which cats are not adverse. It appears that when cats have benign digestive problems, they willingly eat couch grass.

Living with "Neighbor" Cats

If you are fortunate enough to live in an individual house, there will invariably be problems with cohabitation. Generally, cats resolve these problems rather well, although often noisily. But the fury and noise worthy of Shakespeare that pussycats can unleash at night should not cause their owner to tremble. This is a bluffing strategy that cats push to the limits.

The bites, scratches and abscesses that may result are more frequent with full-grown males than with other cats. Neutering or spaying is always advisable because this operation protects the cat from numerous infectious diseases, some of which can be lethal. This operation can be performed starting at the age of six months (or even a little earlier, depending on the development and maturity of the cat and the season. Female cats that are five months old in January will be much more pre-

Mixed breed in a tree trunk

Angora Turk in a garden.

BRUSHING

For short or medium-haired breeds, you can use a curry-comb, which will really separate the fur. For longhaired breeds, now is the time to do a brushing with a soft brush.

Brushing helps restore the fullness and fluffiness of the fur.

Bathing will change the appearance of the coat and it will take two days for the fur to regain its natural consistency.

Cats then provide the "finishing touches" themselves, with the grooming tool nature gave them – their tongue. It is sometimes necessary to limit their enthusiasm, especially with longhaired breeds. Indeed, licking too heavily in one area of the coat can cause the fur to become tangled and stuck together. In this case, the best solution is to put a collar on the cat (which can be quite elegant) until it is time to show the cat during a contest.

cocious than cats that turn five months old in November). The procedure also helps prevent overpopulation and needless problems with the neighbors.

Gardeners, Take Pity on Slugs and Mice

Many products commonly used by gardeners are toxic for cats. Unfortunately, even gardeners who love cats often find themselves in a bind when they underestimate a cat's abilities to go exploring in narrow, hard to reach places. As a precaution (this also applies to children), it is better to ban rat and slug killers from the garden for good.

Hygiene

House-Training

Some cats are so meticulous with their litter box that the owner is forced to change the litter after every use.

American Shorthair in its litter box

Without exaggerating, the litter box should be checked every day and maintained according to the type of litter used. Bentonite or sepiolite-based litters have the distinctive feature of clumping around urine to form small balls that can be periodically removed at least every three days. Feces remain intact and are removed in the same manner with a small shovel. The advantage of this type of litter is that it limits odors that not only bother owners (and their guests), but also the user(s) of the litter box. Odors that are too strong will repel the cat and sometimes lead him to answer the call of nature in a less appropriate, albeit more inviting, place (shower stall, bathtubs, flower pots, etc.).

Traditional, non-clumping litter needs to be changed every day.

For longhaired cats, it is recommended to trim the hair around the anus so as to avoid the nasty surprise of finding feces stuck there.

Coat Maintenance

Even for shorthaired cats, weekly or even daily brushing is a good way to check the cat to see if all is well and that there are no little wounds, parasites, etc. In this way, cats generally get a little tender loving care of a slightly different kind. With longhaired cats, brushing is imperative. Kittens must be taught young to tolerate the session, which should never end with scratching. If the cat is not patient enough, several short brushing sessions could be done. Purebred cats that will be shown on a regular basis, must be trained at a young age to tolerate being handled and bathed. Go easy during the first bath and be attentive to any signs of anxiety so as not to create any aversions in the future champion. Unfortunately, aversions can be instilled very quickly.

For cats with outdoor access, it is necessary to be vigilant especially in spring, when cats shed their hair and when the rainy season hits with full force. Longhaired cats, even if they spend a long time grooming themselves, are not sheltered from having their hair become matted and compacted into sometimes voluminous masses. These mats then become an inviting

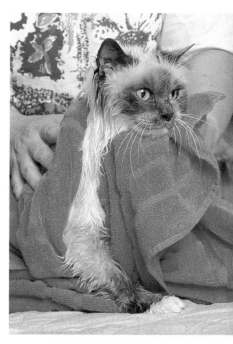

Grooming of a Burmese Sacred Cat

spot for parasites, which cause serious dermatological problems. Be sure to get to the groomer and the veterinarian in time (a general anesthesia may sometimes be necessary).

It is normal to find whiskers from time to time on pillows, the sofa or other places where the cat is used to sleeping. There is no cause for concern. Cat whiskers are a particular type of hair but are shed more slowly than hair.

Eyes and Ears

The eyes should only be cleaned if they are watery and even then, it is always preferable to seek the advice of a veterinarian before applying a cleaning product. In fact, epiphora (watering) does not normally occur in cats. If watering does occur, it may be an indication of a problem with the tear glands or eyelids, or an infectious or viral disease. Persian cats, whose faces are very flat, require frequent eye care. Use products recommended by your veterinarian.

The ears should not be cleaned unless you notice the presence of yellowish or brownish deposits. If your cat is scratching its ear furiously or tilting its head, you should take it to the veterinarian as soon as possible and refrain from using any product that could conceal a foreign object. Never use cotton swabs (which would only push the foreign object further into the eardrum) and ask your veterinarian what products to use.

Teeth

Ear care on a Maine Coon kitten

At four months old, cats begin to get their adult teeth, especially the fangs, which have a different morphology from baby teeth.

It is almost illusory to try to brush cats' teeth. However, you should regularly check the color of the teeth and look for possible tartar buildup. Regular crunching promotes chewing and prevents tartar buildup, or at least limits buildup if it has already started. Therefore, do not

Show cats are required to have their claws trimmed or they will be disqualified. The best way to trim the claws seems to be to sit down and to hold the cat in between your thighs on its back. Reassure the cat by petting his stomach between every few cuts.

Using guillotine clippers, trim the tip of the claw, staying well above the pink triangle, which is fleshy part of the claw matrix. Cutting any lower will cause heavy bleeding and a pain that the cat will remember during the next session.

If your cat is used to this operation, it will integrate it as part of the ritual process with you and trimming its nails before a show will not be a problem.

You can also take advantage of this opportunity to trim the hair growing between your Persian's digits.

Trimming the claws of an Abyssinian

deprive your cat of the pleasure of eating dry food. Accustom it to eating dry food and to drinking fresh water at a young age. If the tap water is hard water, mineral water is recommended. Your veterinarian will check the state of the teeth during annual check-ups and if necessary, suggest de-scaling, which is a mild treatment requiring a brief anesthesia.

Claws

The act of scratching objects is part of normal behavior for cats. However, this behavior does not always fit well with sedentary apartment life. Indeed, although scratching trees is not a problem for the owner of a cat that has free access to the yard, scratching the leather sofa or expensive furniture can seriously compromise community life.

When cats have to live in apartments, it is important to forbid them from scratching objects you do not want them to scratch, starting at a young age. A simple "no" along with a sharp noise (clapping your hands) will suffice to correct this behavior. If a young kitten exhibits this behavior often, especially upon waking, you should give it one or more objects that can be used as a scratching post. Cats do not always accept commercial scratching posts. Often a piece of wood (birch, pine, and even olivewood) will do the trick better. Scratching posts should be changed regularly since cats eventually grow weary of them.

"De-clawing" a cat involves a mutilating surgical operation since it consists of amputating the last phalanx of the cat's front paws, definitively removing the claw and its root (the claw is equivalent to human fingernails, which cannot be removed without their base). This operation should not be performed without first discussing all the aspects with your veterinarian.

Various studies have shown that this ablation does not compromise the cat's hunting and jumping abilities. In Quebec, this operation is widely practiced and cats there do not seem to have any particular problems with motor functions. However, bear in mind that depending

on the nature of the cat, scratching, along with vocal sounds and characteristic growling, is a means of advertising or issuing a warning about impending aggression (biting). Cats with agile paws, who can no longer use scratching to defend themselves after being operated on, have been known to start biting without going through any other process.

Claws should be trimmed approximately every three to four weeks, for cats that do not get exercise. It is better to have two people, one to hold the cat down without force and one to look closely at the claw before trimming it. Special clippers are sold at veterinarian offices. It is important not to cut the living tissue part of the claw or it will start to bleed. In order to spare you cat, it is perhaps wise to accustom it gradually to these manicure sessions and to ask your veterinarian to show you how to proceed.

The Milestones of Life

The Birth of a Child

For a cat that belongs to a couple, the birth of a baby is a major event that will necessarily change the relationship. Indeed, despite all the good intentions of the owner, the cat will never again have the same relationship with the couple.

Before the birth, it is important to start accustoming the cat to no longer having access to the nursery, especially if the cat was in the habit of roaming in the apartment or house freely without restriction.

During your stay at the maternity ward, think about giving the baby's first blankets to the father. He can take them home and leave them out in the open in a small basket. The odors will give your cat(s) some indications of the new arrival and facilitate introductions.

When you come home from the hospital, think about taking the time to make introductions. Both the baby and the cat will be sensitive to what you say and understand more than you might think.

Later on, be sure to continue paying attention to the cat and try not to only shower him with affection when your baby is sleeping (or he will associate the absence of the baby with an abundance of attention). Rather, you should pet him and talk to him in front of your baby, which will also help the baby become a cat lover later on.

The temptation for cats to adopt babies sometimes pushes them to risky behavior, such as wanting to sleep in the cradle. Indeed, the cradle is a warm, pleasant place, sometimes with the delicious aroma of curdled milk (your cat does not necessarily have the same opinion of regurgitation as you do!). Be careful therefore to channel your cat's impulses by possibly giving him doll cradle of his own.

As the baby grows and depending on the nature of the cat, you will generally be surprised to see how tolerant the cat is vis-à-vis your child (a tolerance that is generally limited only to the child or children of the family). The cat is a wonderful source of life lessons for the child. Around the age of 15 months for example, the child will start to discover that the cat has a funny tail. A simple growl from the cat is enough to make the child understand that respect for individuals is important. However, during this age when the child is discovering everything fearlessly, you need to be vigilant and always ensure mutual respect.

Moving

Moving is a big event for cats, who are sometimes said to be more attached to places than people. Some cats prove this by returning to their old house, sometimes making very long journeys. There was one old cat, for instance, that in all likelihood made the roundtrip between Lyon and Barcelonette, in the South of France, disappointed to find its old house abandoned.

During the move, it is wise to lock the cat in one room with food, a litter box and a few toys. If possible, wait until the very last to bring the cat and put him in a room that is relatively arranged.

A move between two different apartments generally does not pose a problem. The cat will quickly take possession of its new territory.
If the cat is moving from a house to an apartment, plan to arrange the apartment so that it can jump and climb in order to help it become accustomed to being deprived of freedom and access to the outside.

If the cat moves from an apartment to a house, it is wise not to let it outside for three to seven days and thereafter to monitor it when it goes outside, either by watching or going outside with it. From then on, let it go outside more and more frequently, but keep a box of cat food nearby to bring it back!

Vacations

Cats really do not like to travel in cars or any other means of transport. For this reason, it is always better to find a friend who can stop by your house to feed the cat and change the litter, especially for short trips.

If you rent a vacation house, even for a month, your cat will not get used to it unless you take it there regularly, something you can start accustoming it to at an early age. Sometimes a cat's ability to adapt is staggering, such as the case of the cat that got used to travelling with his owner on a motorcycle at an early age.
Some cats that are used to living in an apartment during the year, may be depressed when they return from the vacation in the country in September. If your cat seems to be lacking energy or appetite, or if it starts to urinate inappropriately, do not hesitate to take it to the veterinarian.

TRIPS

Cats may be irritated by travelling in cars, buses or subways, even for short trips (such as going to the veterinarian). Heat, dim light and silence may reassure your cat. Put him in a willow basket cage or even a simple, thick cardboard box for trips (do not worry, he will not suffocate). Line the box with a paper towels and put a cloth under him.
If the cat is emotional, it may have an accident within the first five to ten minutes. If this happens, remove the paper towels so that it may finish the trip dry.
One trick is to place the willow basket in a slightly filled litter box. Urine will then flow through the basket into the litter box, leaving the cat dry. This trick also protects the seats and floor covering in your car. If the trip is long, give the cat food (preferably dry food) and fresh water periodically when you make meal stops. Do not leave food in its cage or box however.
A tranquilizer may be useful for air travel. Consult your veterinarian.

A cat in its transportation basket.

A Sick Cat

Before hospitalizing a cat, even under the best of conditions, the best interests of the cat and the owner's possibilities should always be discussed with the veterinarian. The amount of stress on the cat and the strength of the bond between the cat and its owner are aspects veterinarians specialized in feline medicine will consider as factors that may influence the morale of the animal and its ability to recuperate.

It may be wiser to simply take the cat to the clinic to receive treatment (day hospitalization) unless the owner can come by the clinic once or twice a day to visit his cat and give him food, which the cat often accepts more readily when given with such a loving heart.

Photographs Credits

All photos in this work are from the Cogis agency's photographic archives:
Francais, Garguil, Gauzargues, Gehlmar, Gelhar, Gengoux, Grissey, Hermeline, Ingeborg, Labat, Lanceau, Lepage, Lili, Nicaise, Potier, Remy, Rocher, Schwartz, Seitre, Varin, Vedie, Vidal, Willy's, Zizola.

Except:

- photos from the Royal Canin archives: Philippe Psaïla, Jean-Pierre Lenfant en Yves Renner

Coordination Royal Canin: Catherine Legros
Project Editors: Diffomédia / Paris
Art Director: Guy Rolland
Coordination: Béatrice Fortamps,
assisted by: Céline Davaze and Valérie de Leval
Illustrations: Agnès Pezon
Cover: Somali - © Hermeline/Cogis
© 2003 Aniwa SA

Publisher: Aniwa Publishing
10, rue du Colisée - F.-75008 - Paris
Tel.: + 33 (0)1 44 95 02 20/Fax: + 33 (0)1 44 95 02 22
www.aniwa.com
Copyright: first quarter 2003

Printed in CEE